A BOOKSHOP
IN BERLIN

A BOOKSHOP IN BERLIN

*The Rediscovered Memoir of
One Woman's Harrowing Escape from the Nazis*

Françoise Frenkel

With a preface from PATRICK MODIANO
Dossier compiled by FRÉDÉRIC MARIA
Translated by STEPHANIE SMEE

ATRIA BOOKS

NEW YORK   LONDON   TORONTO   SYDNEY   NEW DELHI

ATRIA
BOOKS

An Imprint of Simon & Schuster, Inc.
1230 Avenue of the Americas
New York, NY 10020

First published in France as *Rien où poser sa tête* by L'Arbalète Gallimard in 2015

Copyright © 2015 by Éditions Gallimard for the "Preface" by Patrick Modiano and the "Dossier" by Frédéric Maria

English translation copyright © 2017 by Stephanie Smee
Originally published in English by Vintage Australia in 2017
Previously published by Pushkin Press in 2018

Pushkin Press has searched for the rightful claimants of Françoise Frenkel's estate. Their rights and royalties have been reserved for them by Pushkin Press.

First Atria Books hardcover edition December 2019

ATRIA BOOKS and colophon are trademarks of Simon & Schuster, Inc.

For information about special discounts for bulk purchases, please contact Simon & Schuster Special Sales at 1-866-506-1949 or business@simonandschuster.com.

The Simon & Schuster Speakers Bureau can bring authors to your live event. For more information or to book an event, contact the Simon & Schuster Speakers Bureau at 1-866-248-3049 or visit our website at www.simonspeakers.com.

Interior design by Kyoko Watanabe

Manufactured in the United States of America

1 3 5 7 9 10 8 6 4 2

Library of Congress Cataloging-in-Publication Data is available.

ISBN 978-1-5011-9984-4
ISBN 978-1-5011-9986-8 (ebook)

Contents

Contents

Preface

The copy of *No Place to Lay One's Head** that was recently found, I'm told, in Nice, in an Emmaus Companions charity jumble sale, had a curious effect on me. Perhaps because it had been printed in Switzerland in September 1945 for Geneva-based publishers Jeheber. That publishing house, now defunct, had in 1942 published *L'aventure vient de la mer,* a French translation of Daphne du Maurier's novel *Frenchman's Creek,* published in London the previous year, one of those English or American novels banned by the Nazi censors but sold covertly and even on the black market in Paris under the Occupation.

We don't know what became of Françoise Frenkel following the publication of *No Place to Lay One's Head.* At the end of her book, she recounts how in 1943 she smuggled herself across the

---

*The original title of this memoir is *Rien où poser sa tête,* or *No Place to Lay One's Head.* This edition is called *A Bookshop in Berlin.*

border into Switzerland from Haute-Savoie. According to the note at the end of the foreword, she wrote *No Place to Lay One's Head* in Switzerland "on the shores of Lake Lucerne, 1943–1944." Sometimes strange coincidences occur: in a letter sent by Maurice Sachs a few months earlier, in November 1942, from a house in the Orne where he had taken refuge, I happen upon the title of Françoise Frenkel's book in the course of a sentence: "It appears it's rather my path, if not my fate, *to have no place to lay my head*."

What was Françoise Frenkel's life like after the war? These are the scarce pieces of information I have been able to gather about her thus far: she recalls, in her account, the French bookshop she had established in Berlin in the early 1920s—the only French bookshop in the city—and which she apparently managed until 1939. In July of that year, facing imminent danger, she abandons Berlin in all haste for Paris. But in Corine Defrance's study La *"Maison du Livre français" à Berlin (1923–1933)* we learn that she ran this bookshop with her husband, a certain Simon Raichenstein, about whom she says not a word in her book. This phantom husband is supposed to have left Berlin for France at the end of 1933 under a Nansen passport. It seems identity papers were denied him by the French authorities, who issued him with a deportation order. But he remained in Paris. He was taken from Drancy to Auschwitz in the convoy of July 24, 1942. He had been born in Russia, in Mogilev, and it appears he lived in the 14th arrondissement.

We find a trace of Françoise Frenkel among the State Archives of the Canton of Geneva in the list of persons recorded at the Geneva border during the Second World War; that is to say, those who were granted permission to remain in Switzerland after crossing the border. That list provides us with her true full name: Raichenstein-Frenkel, Frymeta, Idesa; her date of birth: July 14, 1889; and her country of origin: Poland.

One last trace of Françoise Frenkel, fifteen years later: a compensation claim in her name dated 1958. It refers to a trunk she had left in the Colisée storage repository at 45 Rue du Colisée in Paris in May 1940, and which was confiscated on November 14, 1942, on the grounds it was "Jewish property." In 1960, she is awarded compensation in the sum of 3,500 Deutsch marks for the despoliation of her trunk.

What did it contain? One coypu fur coat. One coat with an opossum collar. Two woolen dresses. A black raincoat. A dressing gown from Grünfeld's. An umbrella. A parasol. Two pairs of shoes. A handbag. An electric heat pad. An Erika portable typewriter. A Universal portable typewriter. Gloves, socks, and handkerchiefs . . .

Do we really need to know more? I don't believe we do. What makes *No Place to Lay One's Head* unique is that we cannot precisely identify its author. This eyewitness account of the life of a woman hunted through the south of France and Haute-Savoie during the Occupation is all the more striking in that it reads like the testimony of an anonymous woman, much as *A Woman in Berlin*—also published in Switzerland in the 1950s—was thought to be for a long time.

If we think back to our first readings of works of literature, around the age of fourteen, we knew nothing of their authors either, whether it was Shakespeare or Stendhal. But that naïve and direct reading left its mark on us forever, as if each book were a sort of meteorite. In this day and age writers appear on television screens and at book fairs; they're constantly interposing themselves between their works and their readers, and turning into traveling salesmen. We miss our childhood years when we would read *The Treasure of the Sierra Madre*, written under the pseudonym B. Traven, a man whose identity remained unknown even to his publishers.

I prefer not to know what Françoise Frenkel's face looked like, nor the twists and turns of her life after the war, nor the date of her death. Thus, her book will always remain for me that letter from an unknown woman, a letter forgotten poste restante for an eternity, that you've received in error, it seems, but that perhaps was intended for you. That curious impression I had upon reading *No Place to Lay One's Head* was also the effect of hearing the voice of somebody whose face one can't quite make out in the half-light and who is recounting an episode from their life. And that reminded me of the overnight trains of my youth, not in the "sleeping cars" but the seated compartments which used to create a great sense of intimacy between passengers, and where somebody, under the night-light, would end up confiding in you or even confessing to you, as if in the privacy of a confessional. It was the feeling that you would no doubt never see each other again that lent weight to this abrupt intimacy. Brief encounters. You retain a suspended memory of them, the memory of somebody who didn't have time to tell you everything. The same can be said of Françoise Frenkel's book, written seventy years ago but in the confusion of the moment, still suffering from shock.

I ended up tracking down the address of the bookshop run by Françoise Frenkel: 39a Passauer Strasse; telephone: Bavaria 20-20, between Schöneberg and Charlottenburg. I imagine them in that bookshop, she and her husband, who is absent from her book. At the time she was writing, she was probably unaware of his fate. Simon Raichenstein had a Nansen passport, since he belonged to that group of émigrés from Russia. There were more than one hundred thousand of them in Berlin in the early 1920s. They had settled in the Charlottenburg neighborhood, which, as a result, had come to be known as "Charlottengrad." Many of these White Russians spoke French, and I assume they were the main customers of Mr. and Mrs. Raichenstein's bookshop. Vladimir Nabokov, who used to live in the area, no doubt one evening crossed the threshold of that bookshop. No need to consult archives or study photos. All you need do, I'm sure, if you want to find a trace of Françoise Frenkel in Berlin, is read Nabokov's Berlin stories and novels, which he wrote in Russian and which are the most moving of his works. You can picture her on the crepuscular avenues and in the poorly lit apartments of Nabokov's descriptions. Leafing through *The Gift*, Nabokov's last Russian novel and a farewell to his mother tongue, you come across the description of a bookstore which must have resembled that of Françoise Frenkel and the enigmatic Simon Raichenstein. "Crossing Wittenberg Square, where, as if in a colour film, roses trembled in the breeze around an old-fashioned stairway that descended into an underground station, he made his way towards the bookshop . . . the lights were still on . . . Books were still being sold to taxi drivers on the nightshift, and he made out, through the yellow opacity of the shop-window, the silhouette of Misha Berezovski . . ."

In the last fifty pages of her book, Françoise Frenkel recounts a first failed attempt to cross the Swiss border. She is taken to the police station in Saint-Julien together with "two girls in tears, a dazed-looking little boy, and a woman worn out from exhaustion and cold." The following day she is transferred by bus, together

with other fugitives who had been arrested, to the prison in
Annecy.

I find these pages moving, having spent many years in this
part of Haute-Savoie. Annecy, Thônes, the Glières Plateau,
Megève, Le Grand-Bornand . . . Memories of the war, of resistance fighters, lived on during my childhood and adolescent
years. Fingerprints. Handcuffs. She appears before a tribunal of
sorts. As luck would have it, she is given a "minimum suspended
sentence and pronounced free." The next day she is released
from custody. On leaving the prison, she walks in the sunshine
through the streets of Annecy. I am familiar with the path she
happens to take. She hears the murmur of a fountain that I, too,
used to hear in the silent, stiflingly hot early afternoons on the
shores of the lake at the end of the Pâquier promenade.

Her second attempt to smuggle herself across the Swiss border is a success. I often used to take a bus to Geneva from the
Annecy bus station. I had noticed it would pass through customs
with never any inspection whatsoever. Yet, as it approached the
border, from the Saint-Julien-en-Genevois side, I would feel a
slight tightening within. Perhaps the memory of a sense of menace still hovered in the air.

PATRICK MODIANO

Foreword

It is the duty of those who have survived to bear witness to ensure the dead are not forgotten, nor humble acts of self-sacrifice left unacknowledged.

May these pages inspire a reverent thought for those forever silenced, fallen by the wayside or murdered.

I dedicate this book to the MEN AND WOMEN OF GOOD-WILL who, generously, with unfailing courage, opposed the will to violence and resisted to the end.

Dear reader, accord them the grateful affection deserved by all such magnanimous acts!

In my thoughts, too, are those Swiss friends who took my hand just as I felt myself sinking, and the bright smile of my friend Lie, who helped me continue to live.

F. F.
IN SWITZERLAND,
ON THE SHORES OF LAKE LUCERNE,
1943–1944

A BOOKSHOP
IN BERLIN

A French bookshop in Berlin

I don't know exactly when I first felt the calling to be a book-seller. As a very young girl, I could spend hours leafing through a picture book or a large illustrated tome.

My favorite presents were books, which would pile up on the shelves along the walls of my childhood bedroom.

For my sixteenth birthday, my parents allowed me to order my own bookcase. To the astonishment of the joiner, I designed and had built a cabinet with glass on all four sides. I positioned this piece of furniture, conjured from my dreams, in the middle of my bedroom.

Not wanting to spoil my delight, my mother let me do as I pleased and I was able to admire my classics in the publishers' beautiful bindings, and the modern, contemporary authors whose bindings I would lovingly choose myself, according to my whim.

Balzac came dressed in red leather, Sienkiewicz in yellow morocco, Tolstoy in parchment, Reymont's *Paysans* clad in the fabric of an old peasant's neckerchief.

Later, the cabinet was positioned against the wall, which was covered in a beautiful, bright cretonne fabric, and this move in no way diminished my delight.

And then, time passed . . .

Life had led me to Paris, for long years of study and work.

Every spare moment I had was spent along the riverbanks in front of the *bouquinistes'* old, damp cases of books. Sometimes I would dig up a book from the eighteenth century, in which I was particularly interested at the time. Sometimes I thought I had discovered a document, a rare volume, an old letter; always a fresh, if fleeting, moment of joy.

Such memories!

The Rue des Saints-Pères, with its dusty, dark boutiques, troves of accumulated treasures, what a world of marvelous discoveries! Oh, the bewitching years of my youth!

And time spent lingering on the corner of Rue des Écoles and Boulevard Saint-Michel at that huge bookshop that used to spill out onto the footpath. Works with uncut pages, skimmed through amid the noise of the street: horns honking, students and girls chatting and laughing, music, snatches of popular songs . . .

We readers were far from distracted by this hustle and bustle, which was part of our student life. If that commotion had disappeared and those voices had fallen silent, it would quite simply have been impossible to keep reading on the corner of the boulevard: a peculiar sense of oppression would have weighed upon us all . . .

But happily there was no such thing to worry about then. Certainly, the war had reduced the pitch of our general gaiety by a few tones, but Paris was alive with its animated, insouciant atmosphere. The Latin Quarter rippled with youth, street corners still hummed with song, and book lovers continued their furtive reading in front of tables laden with treasures provided so generously to everybody by publishers and booksellers, with friendly goodwill, and no thought of profit.

◇◇◇

At the end of the first war, I returned to my hometown. After my first outpourings of delight at finding my loved ones safe and sound, I hurried to my childhood bedroom.

I stopped in my tracks, astonished. The walls had been stripped: the floral cretonne had been skillfully peeled off and removed. All that remained were newspapers stuck up against the plaster. My beautiful library with its four glass panels, the wonder of my youthful imagination, stood empty, seemingly ashamed of its own decadence.

The piano, too, had disappeared from the drawing room.

Everything had been taken away under the Occupation of 1914–1918.

But my family was alive and well. I spent a happy holiday in their midst and returned to France full of vim and vigor.

When I didn't have lectures at the Sorbonne, I studied diligently at the Bibliothèque Nationale, as well as at the Sainte-Geneviève Library, my favorite place.

Upon my return from Poland, I worked in the afternoons at a bookstore in Rue Gay-Lussac.

Over time I grew to know my bookish clientele. I would try

to fathom their desires, understand their tastes, their beliefs, and their leanings, try to guess at the reasons behind their admiration of, their enthusiasm for, their delight or displeasure with a work.

By and by, after observing the way a book was held, almost tenderly, the way pages were delicately turned and reverently read or hastily and thoughtlessly leafed through, the book then put back on the table, sometimes so carelessly that its corners, its most precious part, were damaged as a result, I came to be able to see into a character, a spirit, a state of mind. I would place the book I considered appropriate down close to a reader—discreetly, however, so they wouldn't feel it had been suggested to them. If they happened to like it, I glowed.

I started to grow fond of my customers. When they left the shop, I found myself walking with them a little way in my imagination. I wondered about the impact the book they had taken would have on them; then, I would impatiently await their return to hear their thoughts.

But there were other times, too . . . when the sheer intellectual vandalism of a customer would drive me to distraction. For there were some people who desecrated a work, heaping it with angry criticism and objections, until its contents were quite falsely distorted!

I have to admit, much to my bewilderment, that it was more often women who were guilty of this lack of moderation.

Thus I had discovered the necessary complement to a book: its reader.

Generally speaking, a perfect harmony reigned between one and the other in the little store on Rue Gay-Lussac.

Every spare moment I had was spent at publishers' showrooms, where I would go to discover old acquaintances as well as new releases, objects of surprise and delight.

When the time came for me to choose a profession, I didn't hesitate: I followed my calling to be a bookseller.

◇◇◇

It was December 1920 . . . I was off to pay one of my customary short visits to my relatives. On the way there, I stopped in Poznań, Warsaw, then, after holidaying with my family, I went to Kraków.

In my suitcase I was carrying the first two volumes of *Les Thibaults* by Roger Martin du Gard, *Les Croix de bois* by Dorgelès, and *Civilisation* by Duhamel, books I thought would best convey my admiration for the rich flourishing of postwar French literature to the friends and booksellers I intended to meet.

My plan was to open a bookshop in Poland. I visited those three cities, one after the other, and saw that booksellers everywhere were displaying handsome collections of French books. There did not seem to be any demand for another French bookshop.

I decided to stop briefly in Berlin on my return journey in order to see friends there, and then to take the night train, which would arrive in Paris first thing in the morning.

As we wandered along Berlin's grand boulevards I loitered, as I was wont to do, in front of the window displays of the big bookshops. We had walked down Unter den Linden, Friedrichstrasse, and Leipziger Strasse when I exclaimed:

"But you don't have any French books!"

"That's quite possible," came the reply, laconic and indifferent.

We resumed our promenade, retracing our steps, and this time I went into the bookshops. Everywhere I was assured that demand for French books was almost nonexistent. "We have a few classics in stock."

Newspapers and journals? Not a trace. Vendors in their newsstands responded ungraciously to my inquiries.

Left with this impression, I returned to Paris.

Professor Henri Lichtenberger, to whom I recounted the outcome of my travels, said to me simply:

"Well then, why don't you go and open a bookshop in Germany?"

One publisher exclaimed, "Berlin? Now that's a major city! Why don't you try your luck?"

My dear professor and friend, P——, announced, "A French bookshop in Berlin . . . you could almost call that a crusade."

My sights were not set so high: I was just after an occupation, that of bookseller, the only one that mattered to me. The Berlin I had glimpsed through the winter fog was sprawling, sad, and morose, but the prospect of working there was not without its attractions.

It was in this frame of mind that shortly afterward I headed back to Germany's capital.

◇◇◇

My first step was to approach the French Consulate General, where I outlined my plans with all the enthusiasm of my convictions, emphasizing the moral support I'd already garnered.

The Consul General raised his arms heavenward:

"But madame, it seems you are unaware of the current moral climate in Germany! You don't appreciate the true state of affairs! If you knew the difficulties I already face just keeping on a few French teachers here. Our newspapers are only sold in a few rare newsstands. French people come all the way to the Consulate just to get hold of them, and you want to open an entire bookshop? They'll burn it to the ground!"

I discovered later that the Consulate in Breslau had been ransacked by a German mob after the plebiscite in Upper Silesia.

At the French Embassy, I was only able to meet with a young attaché; he was hardly more encouraging. But after a week of inquiries and some consideration, I had made my decision: there were no French books to be had in all Berlin, a capital city, a university town where you could already feel the pulse of new life. Given time, a French bookshop would surely succeed.

To me, Germany was not a complete unknown. I had spent some time there as a girl to perfect my German and to pursue my music studies with Professor Xaver Scharwenka.

I later had a second stay in Germany and enrolled in a semester of courses at the Leipzig University for Women.

I was not unfamiliar with the great German masters, the country's thinkers, poets, and musicians. And with their influence in mind, I had every hope my bookshop in the capital might succeed.

Of course, in such a bureaucratic city I had to complete numerous administrative formalities before I could get started. The first civil servant I saw in Berlin revealed himself to be firmly opposed to the sale of exclusively French books. We managed to agree on the description of a *Center for Foreign Books*. My German interlocutor was also of the opinion that it was a bad time to be implementing my plans.

And so, notwithstanding official objections, my attempt to

establish a French bookshop in Berlin saw the light of day. Its first site was on the mezzanine of a private house, in a quiet neighborhood, away from the city center.

Parcels started to pour in from Paris, bringing beautiful volumes with the colorful covers so typical of French publishers; books filled the shelves, climbed all the way to the ceiling, and lay strewn all over the floor.

Scarcely had I finished setting up when customers started to arrive. At first they were mainly women, it's fair to say, and foreigners for the most part, Poles, Russians, Czechs, Turks, Norwegians, Swedes, and numerous Austrians. A visit by a French man or woman was a significant event. There were very few French expatriates remaining. Many who had left on the eve of the Great War had not returned.

It was always a big day for my beautiful female customers when the newspapers and fashion magazines arrived, and they would swoop on them with exclamations of delight, spellbound at the sight of the designs they had been deprived of for so long. The art publications had their ardent admirers too.

My lending library was very well received. Soon readers had to add their names to a waiting list to borrow the books, which were being taken by storm.

Some months later, increasing customer numbers forced me to consider expanding, and the bookshop moved to the capital's fashionable quarter.

1921! This sparkling era was marked by the resumption of international relations and the exchange of ideas. The German *élite* started to make an appearance, very cautiously at first, in this new French literary haven. Then Germans started to appear in ever-increasing numbers: experts in literature and languages, professors, students, and members of that aristocracy whose education had been so strongly influenced by French culture, those who even then were known as "the old generation."

What a curiously mixed clientele. Famous artists, celebrities, well-heeled women pore over the fashion magazines, speaking in hushed tones so as not to disturb the philosopher buried in his Pascal. Next to the window display, a poet leafs reverently through a handsome edition of Verlaine, a bespectacled scholar scrutinizes the catalogue of a bookshop specializing in the sciences, a high school teacher has gathered about him four grammar textbooks, solemnly comparing the chapters grappling with the agreement of participles followed by the infinitive.

I was surprised to realize the extent of German interest in the French language and to see how familiar some of them were with its masterpieces. One high school teacher pointed out to me the dozen or so significant lines missing from the edition of Montaigne he held in his hand. He was right—the edition was abridged. Upon hearing a few lines of a French poet, one expert would be able to say the author's name without hesitation. Another would be able to recite from memory the maxims of La Rochefoucauld, Chamfort, and Pascal's *Pensées*.

This bookseller's life allowed me to mingle with congenial eccentrics. One German customer, a man who knew his grammar, had been on his way out after making a purchase when he'd heard one of my staff saying, "*Au plaisir, monsieur!*" He made an about-face and asked for an explanation of this expression. He wanted to know if it was just a commercial pleasantry, or if one might also use it socially, and in what circumstances, et cetera and so on.

He wrote the expression down in a notebook and thereafter never once failed to offer an "*Au plaisir*," accompanied by a knowing smile on his visits to the shop.

Like harbingers of diplomacy, consulate and embassy staff appeared first; soon they became regular customers. Then came the attachés and, finally, bringing up the rear, *Messieurs*, the diplomats themselves, and above all their wives.

As for His Excellency, the French Ambassador, I received a visit when the bookshop opened in west Berlin.

He thanked me for my initiative, selected several volumes, and in that manner so particular to the French language that combines with ease both firmness and courteous civility, told me that Romain Rolland and Victor Margueritte, one a deserter of the French cause, the other a pornographer, hardly belonged in a self-respecting bookshop. On the other hand, His Excellency did commend to me the works of René Bazin, Barrès, and Henri Bordeaux.

When he had left, I felt both proud and wistful. Despite all my best intentions, I knew it would be impossible for me to take his advice.

The wife of one foreign ambassador, as intelligent as she was lovely, adored browsing through books. She would spend hours looking around and would always discover some volume or other that took her fancy. One day, unafraid to sully her beautifully manicured hands rummaging through the dusty bargains piled high in a back room of the bookshop, she told me quite delightedly:

"Were I not the wife of a diplomat, my dream would be to be a bookseller."

From that day on, our friendship was sealed. I would hunt things down for her from the *bouquinistes* in Paris, she would send customers my way and alert me to the arrival in Berlin of respected French people and celebrities whom we could invite to the lectures and receptions we organized for famous authors passing through Germany.

Claude Anet, Henri Barbusse, Julien Benda, Madame Colette, Dekobra, Duhamel, André Gide, Henri Lichtenberger, André Maurois, Philippe Soupault, Roger Martin du Gard—they all came through the bookshop.

Some of them would give talks. They would speak on literature, art, memories, and impressions; they would attract professors, students, French expatriates, an entire audience of the worldly and well educated. After the lectures we would listen to French records and songs, or readings from poetry and plays.

With the help of willing French people, we also staged "theatrical performances," scenes from Marivaux, Labiche, from *Docteur Knock* by Jules Romains, sometimes even sketches inspired by current events that we ourselves would write. We had as many as five hundred German school students at some performances.

Similarly, the Shrove Tuesday celebrations organized by members of the French community grew to be a significant event for our customers.

In his book *Dix ans après*, Jules Chancel described one of these parties, its atmosphere and what a success it was.

In my work as a bookseller, I had come to enjoy the enlightened support of Professor Hesnard, press attaché and author of an excellent study on Baudelaire. He would help me with his discreet advice.

The cultural attaché who came to Berlin in about 1931 provided infinitely precious support too, and words cannot describe how indebted I am to him for his erudition and loyalty.

In September 1931, I saw Aristide Briand come in, accompanied by an official who was acting as his cicerone. After offering me his congratulations, he inquired whether I had established my business in the spirit of the Franco-German rapprochement. "I do indeed passionately hope for such a rapprochement, just as I hope for a strengthening of relations between all peoples in this world," I replied, "but I established my business here in Berlin on purely intellectual grounds. Politics leads to injustice, blindness, and excess. And following an angry discussion between two customers of differing nationalities, I've always tried to ensure that politics is no longer discussed in the bookshop," I added.

As I watched political events unfolding around me, I had made many an observation in my capacity as a bookseller, witnessed conflicts brewing, sensed the rise of various threats. I would, indeed, have welcomed a chance to speak openly with that great statesman, whose aspirations inspired confidence. But he had company.

Instead, my suspicion of matters political won out. I do not regret not asking Briand any questions, nor having voiced my fears. How quickly was his idealism shattered after that!

I had not opened the Pandora's box at the bottom of which slumbered a ten-millennia-old hope for possible harmony in this world.

◇◇◇

Briand's visit conferred a new prestige upon my bookshop and brought increasing numbers of customers. Years of fellowship, peace, and prosperity followed.

However, starting in 1935, serious complications set in.

First came the question of currency.

In order to pay for my French book orders, I required a new customs authorization each time. I had to provide evidence of the need to import the items. So I gathered references from all sorts of places. Schools issued me with order forms, as did high school teachers. Universities ordered through official channels.

Individual customers completed forms, which I then submitted to the special department responsible for reviewing imported books. To complete my stock, I called on the support of the French Embassy. The work grew laborious.

From time to time, the police would turn up unexpectedly. On the pretext that a particular author was blacklisted, the police officers would inspect everything, confiscating books. Thus they removed copies of Barbusse, later those of André Gide, and, lastly, a great number of other works, among them those of Romain Rolland (who had already been condemned by the French Ambassador).

To fill the gaps created on my shelves, and in an ironic twist, a French correspondent in Berlin reporting for a newspaper from the south of France turned up in the bookshop just at that moment, bringing me his work entitled *En face de Hitler*.* It was . . . Ferdonnet, who was to become wretchedly notorious as a Radio-Stuttgart broadcaster. In self-important tones, he asked me to display a copy of his work in the window. I replied that in accordance with my publishers' instructions, I did not display political works. He replied:

"You do know that I could easily *insist* . . ."

Then, in an imperious tone:

---

* Reference to *Face à Hitler* by Paul Ferdonnet, the French journalist and Nazi sympathizer who was eventually executed for treason in 1945.

"Well, I expect you to sell it nonetheless!"

Police regularly came to confiscate various French newspapers that they had on their list. In turn, this prompted my customers to appear before the shop had opened in order to preempt the inspectors. However, the number of authorized French papers grew increasingly limited.

For several weeks, only *Le Temps* was tolerated. When I heard that all other papers were banned, I rushed immediately to order sufficient copies of it; my customers were desperate for news from abroad. Readers were able to buy it for a week or so. But one fine morning, an inspector informed me that *Le Temps* had now been blacklisted too. He confiscated all of the stock, to the great disappointment of my customers.

Hide newspapers? Keep them under the counter? "Distribution of prohibited newspapers," that would have had me sent to a concentration camp.

From that moment onward, French dailies were no longer available in Germany. They disappeared once and for all.

All these restrictions were the general order of the day.

But with the promulgation of the Nuremberg race laws (at the Party Congress in September 1935), my own personal circumstances became very precarious.

The Nazi Party knew that my bookshop fell, in a manner of speaking, under the protection of French publishers. The German authorities, true to their policy of anesthetizing public opinion, hesitated before causing a scandal. On the one hand, they tolerated my business representing French literature; on the other, they held my origins against me.

My mail included notices, invitations, orders to attend this or that meeting, to take part in that demonstration or Nazi Party rally. Booksellers' associations instructed me to audit my stock and to turn over to the special auditing department any books contravening the spirit of the regime. Attached to all of these forms were questionnaires relating to my race and that of my grandparents and great-grandparents, on both maternal and paternal sides.

In the end, my assistant no longer showed me these depressing documents; he took his motorcycle and made the rounds of government departments, providing them with the requested information. He emphasized my status as a foreigner to iron out difficulties in the short term and to allow me the time to prepare for the winding up of my business.

There were more and more incidents. I remember one affront I was forced to endure a few days before Christmas. Numerous parcels containing gift books had just been delivered by two postmen. Tables were weighed down with beautiful publications for adults, colorful picture books for children. Magazines, reflecting that immaculate French taste unlike anything else in the world, burst from their packaging and were greeted with cries of wonder from the customers.

There was that fever in the air so typical of the time of year!

All of a sudden, the front door of the shop flew open with a crash and the Nazi "block warden" burst in. This gorgon-headed woman was holding two empty tins in each hand.

"Do you speak German?" she shouted.

"Of course," I said, rather astonished.

"These four tins, do they belong to you?"

"I don't know, I'll ask my housekeeper; may I ask why you wish to know?"

"They're yours. I know they are and that's what I'm telling

you! Every German knows there's a container to dispose of tins, and it's not the rubbish bin, it's a special crate with a sign on it! You're going to have a stiff fine to pay! Put that on your Christmas 'bargain' sales account," she added, her eyes full of hatred.

The shrew left. A diplomat who had witnessed the scene told me how, for several days, he had been uncertain as to how to dispose of an aluminum tube bearing the injunction in red: "Do not throw away." He didn't dare put the tube into the wastepaper basket in his hotel room, nor leave it in the street. At last he had the idea of leaving it at a pharmacy, where he was congratulated on behalf of the Party. This anecdote raised a laugh at the time but did not, however, dispel the general feeling of unease.

I was outraged.

Citing the famous "one-pot meal" regulation, the same building superintendent would come to inspect my pots whenever she pleased. She would lift the lids, sniffing the contents, then depart with a Nazi salute.

Furthermore, I owe my first contact with the Gestapo to that woman.

I had taken advantage of the Easter holidays to visit my cousins in Brussels. We had discussed the possibility of moving my bookshop to their city. The result was negative. From there, I had left for Paris, as I did every six months. I was planning to take steps to sell the whole business to French purchasers. My advertisements had appeared in a trade newsletter. A couple agreed to spend a few weeks in Berlin, working in the bookshop, before deciding whether to take on my business.

The day after my return, I was summoned as a matter of urgency to the police station.

On arriving at the Gestapo, I had to pass through three metal gates, each opened, then closed and locked again after me by a man in a black SS uniform. I followed him down long corridors with barred windows. At last he stopped in front of a door and, after knocking, took me into a sort of cell.

Sitting at a table in front of me was a young blond-haired man in uniform: twenty years old, not yet shaving, his face red and blotchy, eyes a washed-out blue, his demeanor furious. He gestured to me to sit down.

"Are you Frau So-and-So? Father's name? Mother's name? Race? Age? Date and place of birth? Identity papers! You are accused of having left at Easter for an unknown destination and of crossing the border illegally."

"I traveled on a normal German exit and reentry visa; I went first to Brussels and then on to Paris."

"Why to Brussels?" he shouted.

"To visit my Belgian relatives."

"What did you take with you when you left? Currency? Gold? Diamonds? You might as well confess, we'll find out in any event!"

He continued to raise his voice and I became increasingly distraught.

"I took nothing of the sort," I replied, holding myself together. "I went to Paris, as I usually do, after stopping first in Belgium, and I returned in accordance with the permit noted in my passport here."

He shoved the passport away, saying:

"Be that as it may! But why exactly did you travel to Brussels by automobile?"

It was obvious he thought he had found the weak point in my journey, and he fixed me with an angry, suspicious stare.

But I had regained my composure.

"I took advantage of some friends traveling to Brussels who offered to drive down the *Autobahn*. I didn't want to leave Germany without having seen this road the whole world is talking about at least once."

"*Ach!* Our *Autobahn* is indeed colossal," agreed the young officer, with a beaming smile that he then furiously suppressed.

"Let's see. You're free to go," he finished off, ever more officious.

I was taken back to the exit. I was *free*!

My friend was waiting for me outside the metal gate. Seeing me, she ran toward me and threw herself into my arms.

Once back at the bookshop, I learned that the French Embassy and the Polish Consulate had telephoned to inquire after me. They had feared the worst.

I've asked myself more than once if I didn't have the famous *Autobahn* to thank for emerging from that affair unscathed, at a time when concentration camps were filling with innocent souls.

As was happening all over the city, nocturnal gatherings of the SA and Brownshirts began taking place in the courtyard of my building, hidden from view. These men would argue about and rail against foreign governments, but they especially had it in for the Jews. They would then launch into hymns glorifying violence, war, hatred, vengeance ...

My four ground-floor window ledges served as seats for these partisans.

What nights of anxious insomnia!

◇◇◇

As I had done so often, I left for two days to visit my family.

My father had departed this world three years earlier. We

had all witnessed his awful agony, powerless to help, despite our every tenderness.

The old home of my childhood, now older still, was in mourning.

My mother was living there with her son, her daughter-in-law, and her grandson, whom she worshipped. She greeted me warmly and showered me with her endless maternal love. My inner torment was calmed just being in her presence.

My mother begged me to abandon my business in order to save myself. Yes, there was nothing else for it.

We would go away together for a while, stay somewhere in our beautiful Polish forests. Later I would find some other way to employ my talents as a bookseller; I would doubtless be successful anywhere.

Thus spoke my mother. I agreed with her wise and loving advice. Everything seemed so straightforward, so easy . . .

◇◇◇

Events followed rapidly, one after the other.

First came the day of the general boycott.

Nazi guards were posted in front of Jewish shops with orders to notify customers that it was contrary to National Socialist policy to patronize shopkeepers of this race. Foreign-owned businesses that had escaped the honor of such a guard remained closed in solidarity.

I kept to my apartment. Suddenly, my housekeeper arrived, looking very nervous.

"Come quickly, madame! They're vandalizing the shop window!"

And indeed, armed with a container of glue and a long paintbrush, boys from the "Hitler Youth" were busy plastering my window with offensive posters.

"What do you think you're doing?" I exclaimed.

"We're carrying out orders."

"Well, stop it at once!"

One of the lads shot a glance at the window displays and said:

"Wait a minute, this is a foreign business. No point carrying on, boys. Let's go!"

It was a gloriously bright, sunny day. I headed toward the main thoroughfares in nearby neighborhoods to try to determine the extent of these activities.

It was at once grotesque and pitiful.

Everywhere the orders were being rigorously and systematically implemented. One scene I witnessed, among many, was almost comical. A lady approaching the entrance to a fashion boutique was warned by the two Nazi guards that it was a Jewish establishment.

"But I'm Jewish too," she said as she stepped up to the door.

"Wait," ordered one of the two watchdogs, catching her by the arm.

They consulted each other, then one of them raced off to seek instructions as to how to deal with this unexpected situation.

A crowd was gathering, awaiting the verdict.

Feigning indifference, the lady had turned her attention to the hats in the window.

A quarter of an hour later, the messenger returned and allowed her to enter the shop.

The boycott that day had been instituted with strict orders to maintain public order. Aside from gatherings on the footpaths, there were no serious incidents.

Everywhere there were people looking embarrassed, almost ashamed; but nobody protested openly . . .

◇◇◇

November 10, 1938, was the unforgettable day of the great pogrom throughout all of Germany.

When news of the death of vom Rath, attaché to the German Embassy in Paris, spread through Berlin in the evening papers, everybody realized that terrible events would follow. People knew that the Party had prepared "reprisals on a grand scale" in advance.

I had spent the evening with friends. We were all feeling miserable and anxious. Returning very late, I heard the raised voices of a big SA meeting in the courtyard.

I went to bed without turning on any lights. I was woken by a strange sound coming from the street. My little clock showed four o'clock. The unusual noise was growing louder and appeared to be getting closer. I recognized the sound as that of a water pump.

I dressed hurriedly, thinking there must be a fire somewhere nearby. I left the house.

Opposite my building and all down the street, firemen were hard at work. The furrier's boutique was burning. Three buildings further down, it was the stationer's; further away still, other fires burned red in the night. I stood rooted to the spot, aghast.

"The synagogue is alight," came the whisper from one group.

I made my way down the street. It was true; the synagogue, housed within a large building, was in flames. Firemen were hosing neighboring houses to prevent the blaze spreading.

"The synagogue is lost!" announced an authoritarian voice in the darkness.

The heat was tremendous. As I left the courtyard, I stumbled on a metal object. It was a silver seven-branched candelabrum, broken and twisted, tossed away.

Out on the street, scattered papers lay strewn all over the ground.

"Public announcements," I thought, bending down to pick up a sheet.

Imagine my astonishment when I saw it was a fragment of Torah scroll, its scattered remains tossed to the winds.

Just then, an old fellow approached the temple. Holding a basket, he started gathering up these scraps of paper covered with Hebrew characters. His lips were moving. He seemed to be reciting a prayer. It was the temple's beadle.

Silently, others from the neighborhood joined him in picking up the desecrated relics, a sorrowful and pathetic group of shadows.

Dawn was breaking.

Tired, I returned home.

Just then, I heard a cry from a window:

"Here comes round two."

Two individuals, armed with long metal bars, suddenly appeared, marching quick time. They were stopping in front of various shop windows and smashing them in. There was a shattering of glass. One of them would then climb into the window displays, kicking and trampling all over the merchandise. Then they would be on their way.

I saw them approaching, heading in my direction.

I found myself on the steps of the bookshop. My heart was beating at a furious pace, my nerves stretched taut. I felt a surge of strength.

They stopped.

One of them spelled out the sign on my shop while the other consulted his list.

"Wait! Wait! It's not on here."

They moved on.

I was left standing there. Had it been necessary, I felt, I would have defended each volume with every ounce of my strength, my life even, driven by devotion to my bookshop, yes, but above all by an immense revulsion for humanity, for life itself, and by an infinite longing for death.

Sitting on the steps of my shop, I waited . . .

Fires were crackling and firefighters still toiling away.

The footpaths and street were littered with all sorts of objects.

Somebody took me by the arm and made me return home.

The city burned like Nero's Rome that day, engulfed in an atmosphere of destruction.

Goods and wares which had been hurled out of windows were carried off by the mob. Whoever tried to defend himself or to save his property was manhandled and abused.

This time, there were bloody, murderous encounters. Everything took place under the very noses of an uninterested police force.

Right next door to these scenes of looting, officers were directing traffic.

The whole city took on an indescribable appearance. Pieces of furniture, pianos, chandeliers, typewriters, piles of stock lay strewn over footpaths; the street was covered with broken windows and mirrors.

Jewelers' and humble working-class shops alike were plundered. Apart from a few commercial enterprises belonging to foreign Jews, everything was destroyed in this sinister and organized fashion.

Hundreds of meters of fabric hung from department store windows, emblems of abomination and savagery.

◇◇◇

The next day, I did not open the bookshop. At around midday, I received a telephone call from a senior official from the Chamber of Commerce. He enjoined me, perfectly politely, to reopen as quickly as possible. He added, by way of aside, that it was not the government's intention to force the closing of foreign businesses; that might have repercussions on German businesses operating outside the country.

During the course of the following day, numerous customers came by to visit me. They brought me flowers and expressed their support. The telephone did not stop ringing. People were asking after me and inquiring about the fate of the bookshop.

Flowers! How sinisterly ironic they seemed, bringing home the full horror of my circumstances! These displays of friendship were nonetheless a comfort to me.

◇◇◇

I had long given up the idea of selling my bookshop. All my efforts in that regard had come to nought. Any interested parties were asking themselves very serious questions! Could a French bookshop survive in Berlin? Wouldn't one be putting oneself in a very difficult position vis-à-vis the National Socialist authorities by purchasing a business that was essentially French? The same problem reared its head once again in 1939, just as it had in 1921 on my reconnaissance trip: was there any point to a French bookshop in Berlin? Those few friends of the bookshop who wished to purchase it were justifiably hesitant and concerned.

As for French purchasers, they came "to see the situation firsthand" and departed again after a few days at most. The young couple who had come from Paris had demonstrated their goodwill, but despite attempts on both sides to reach agreement, their enthusiasm had waned, and first the young woman, then her husband announced that they could not possibly live in such a heavy, joyless atmosphere. Ultimately, I had to face the facts; the bookshop was now redundant and out of place in Germany.

I had still not settled my obligations with respect to the publishing houses. They had placed complete confidence in me and had facilitated my task. It was impossible for me just to close up shop.

In June 1939, a list of my outstanding debts was drawn up and signed off in Paris. The invoices were audited by the Contracts Office (Customs Division: compliance with importation regulations); they then passed through the clearing office before reaching the Reichsbank, accompanied by a payment order.

As this involved the interests of French publishers, these formalities were handled by the Commercial Division of the French Embassy.

On August 1, 1939, I was granted clearing authorization, and I feverishly made the payments.

I tried to find a safe place to store my stock of books. While I was working to make arrangements in this regard—without success, moreover—the atmosphere was growing heavy with menace and danger.

I had attended the Polish Consulate on several occasions in July to inquire about the situation.

Each time I was thoroughly reassured.

The consul admitted to me in confidence that England was in the process of *ironing out* complications that had cropped up in Germano-Polish relations.

On August 25, having settled all my obligations, and on the eve of departing on holiday to visit my family, I returned to the Commercial Division seeking information about the protection of my bookstore. I was concerned to hear that the Polish border was "momentarily" closed, following an exchange of fire between units of the two countries.

To the anxious crowd that had hastily gathered, the reply was given: "Everything will work out, there'll be no war!"

On August 26, I was called to the French Consulate. There I received advice to go to Paris "for the time being," and to take the train that, in twenty-four hours' time, would be transporting French nationals as well as some foreigners from Berlin.

"This mass departure is only a protest against the Nazi violation of the Polish border."

Once again I returned to my consulate. "England is taking action! America is getting involved! Roosevelt will appeal to the German people for peace." My contact, a high-ranking official, added: "However, in your situation, in these troubled times, you are particularly exposed. Why wouldn't you accept the benevolent offer to go to Paris 'temporarily,' and be ready to travel to Poland as soon as conflict is averted? It's a matter of a few days! The Allies are not in the least bit inclined to go to war . . ."

It was said in a tone of profound conviction.

It was later established that the English, French, and Polish diplomats were reluctant to acknowledge the approaching disaster.

That very evening, two devoted friends came over to "pack my bags." Nothing was supposed to leave Germany at that time without express authorization. A multitude of questionnaires had to be filled out, itemizing each object one intended to take: articles of underwear, clothing, shoes, and even scissors, bars of soap, toothbrushes.

I had not considered complying with this formality.

My two friends insisted I take at least some of my personal effects with me. Thanks to them, a trunk was packed.

Huddled up in a corner of the sofa, I left them to it. All my energy had disappeared. It was as if I'd been stunned.

Very late at night, two young people came to take the trunk to the station. Such unusual behavior exposed them to real danger. But they took the risk notwithstanding my protestations.

I was left alone with my bookshop. I watched over it through the night, thinking back on our community, our solidarity, our years of effort and exhilarating struggles.

I saw my customers and friends again before me . . . how, with each of my attempts to leave, they had been so deeply affected. "The bookshop," they used to say, "is the only place we're able to come to rest our minds. Here we can forget and find solace, we can breathe easy. We need it more than ever. Stay!"

That night, I understood how I had been able to withstand the oppressive atmosphere of those last years in Berlin . . . I loved my bookstore the way a woman loves, that is to say, truly.

It had become my life, my raison d'être.

Dawn caught me sitting in my usual spot at my worktable, surrounded by books.

The bookshop seemed almost unreal in the first light of day.

Then I rose to say my farewells . . .

I went from shelf to shelf, tenderly stroking the spines of the books . . . I leaned over the limited editions. How many times had I been too attached, refusing to sell one or another of them!

I re-read the authors' dedications. Some of them were no longer with us. Not Claude Anet . . . How enthusiastically he had spoken of his life in Russia! Nor Henri Barbusse . . . He had shared his memories of Romania, of Russia and Lenin . . . Nor Crevel, young, whimsical, unsettling in his enthusiasm and pessimism.

Some dedications conjured up a moment of camaraderie, others were a fleeting tribute . . . All these treasures had to be left behind. Whose hands would take care of them?

I searched my books for solace and encouragement.

And suddenly I heard an infinitely delicate melody . . . It was coming from the shelves, the display cabinets, from wherever the books were playing out their mysterious life.

I stood there, and listened . . .

It was the voice of the poets, their brotherly attempt to console me in my distress. They had heard their friend's appeal and were offering their farewells to the poor bookseller, stripped of her kingdom.

The first sounds of day brought me back to reality.

◇◇◇

I took the train with the French expatriates, embassy and consulate staff, a few Poles, and other foreigners who were returning to Paris.

Despite the optimistic assurances we had received, most of us thought that conflict was inevitable. We were all overwhelmed, thinking about a future all the more easily envisaged with the events of 1914–1918 in the not-so-distant past.

I had my final run-in with the Nazis at the border. In Cologne, every passenger had to file past a Reichsbank official in order to exchange the maximum sum allowed of ten marks for French currency.

A Polish priest was ahead of me. After a glance at his passport, the German official announced: "Polish! . . . No currency . . . next!"

It was my turn: an equally swift glance at my papers: "Non-Aryan! . . . No currency . . . next!"

It was Nazi Germany's parting word.

On arriving in Paris that evening, I had to call my family from the Gare du Nord station and wait for my relatives to come to collect me; I had no money to take a taxi.

Nazi policy had thus succeeded in reaching beyond the border to strike me . . .

But only a pale foreshadowing of what was to follow.

Fortunately, indeed, I was not to know that then.

Three days after my arrival, I went to inquire after the fate of my trunk. The station employee told me that luggage was not arriving from Germany "for the time being." Nonetheless, he went off to check.

"You're in luck, it was the last one in."

He stamped the docket and added, good-naturedly:

"Keep that as a souvenir, it's a real good-luck charm."

◇◇◇

Some Germans were abandoning their homeland, their fortunes, and their businesses so as not to be complicit in the actions of the National Socialists; others hunkered down behind the walls of their houses to preserve their freedom of thought and action.

Some brave souls spoke out, among them Pastor Niemöller, Father Mayer, Monsignor von Galen, the Bishop of Münster, Cardinal Faulhaber, from Munich, and so many others. Almost all of them disappeared or, like the Jews, were sent to fill the concentration camps.

Their memory, certainly, must not be erased . . .

I also find myself thinking of "the regulars," those faithful friends of the bookshop. What had become of them? Did the tidal wave sweeping away the impetus toward freedom and justice carry off these *men and women of goodwill*?

With profound sadness, I fear so . . .

When I think of the last tumultuous years of my time in Berlin, I see once again a series of stupefying events: the first silent parades of the future Brownshirts; the trial that followed the burning of the Reichstag, typical of National Socialist methods; the rapid transformation of German children into the restless larvae of the Hitler Youth; the masculine rhythm of the blond, blue-eyed girls whose aggressive marching made windowpanes rattle, causing books in window displays to tremble in a somber foreshadowing; the visit of that German mother who wept for her child who had just been congratulated and held up as an example before his whole class because he had denounced her for her anti-Nazi opinions; that other mother, this one Jewish, her heart overflowing with sorrow, who told me her boy, son of a Christian father, had run into her in the street in the company of his Hitler-following friends, and had pretended not to recognize her; the mounting desolation of all mothers faced with the loss of their children as they were wrenched from the family home; the influence of block wardens who intervened in the lives of tenants, denouncing them before the people's courts, dislocating the bonds of marriage, friendship, affection, and love; people stripped first of their professions and positions, then of their wealth, and finally of their civil and human rights; the flight of the persecuted to the borders; the burials of those desperate souls who had thrown themselves under trains or out of windows; the permanent disappearances in concentration camps; the return, after long absences, of customers—such elegant and enlightened minds—heads shorn like convicts, anxious, with faraway expressions and trembling hands. How they had aged in a matter of months!

Oh, the memory of the emergence of a leader with the face of an automaton, a face so deeply marked by hate and pride, dead to all feelings of love, friendship, goodness, or pity . . .

And clustered around this leader with his hysterical voice, a captive crowd capable of any violence, any murderous act!

What an image, the birth of this monstrous and ever-growing human termite colony spreading swiftly through the country with a sinister grinding of metal; a colony with the potential for incalculable collective strength.

II

Paris

In France, nobody believed war was approaching. I breathed in the air of the capital. Very swiftly, I allowed myself to be won over by the general feeling of confidence. I found myself hopeful of an imminent departure and of being reunited with my family.

Throughout these days of heightened crisis, Paris retained its usual outward appearance: movement, color, vitality.

People were discussing the situation on the café terraces, on street corners. In the metro, they would read their neighbor's newspaper over their shoulder; the need to communicate and, if possible, to discover any fresh details from somebody who was perhaps better informed, spurred people to speak to anybody they encountered, to stop in the street to listen, to look, to discuss matters endlessly.

The general public would wait outside the printers' to buy

the papers, ink still wet from the presses. The crowd would jostle to snatch up any new issue; news vendors on their bicycles seemed to sprout wings as they flew down the street. People queued up in front of the newsstands well before the arrival of the newspaper couriers. Some would take several papers, of differing opinion, scour them feverishly on the spot, then pass them on to other readers.

At times the mainstream broadsheets would reassure the population; at other times they encouraged people to prepare for the inevitable.

Radios blared relentlessly in homes, courtyards, squares, offices, restaurants, and cafés. It was impossible to escape their hold. Their rasping tones permeated everywhere, even into theaters, and into the intervals of classical music concerts.

People listened haphazardly to bulletins in any language. A true tower of Babel! Some made certain to wake up in the middle of the night to listen to American broadcasts. It was an obsession! Nervous tension grew to indescribable levels in those days.

Utterly consumed by a fervent desire for peace, the French people were *hoping*. The notorious phrase: *Last year, too, we expected the worst and yet everything worked out* . . . circulated from mouth to mouth, like the chorus of a popular song.

Which is why, when hostilities broke out, the whole of France was plunged into dark despair.

For me, it was heartrendingly distressing.

Only then did I truly comprehend the distance separating me from my mother. I saw myself remaining far from her and all my loved ones for the duration of the war, that is for an eternity of torment and worry about them.

The German army was advancing, trampling over Poland and taking control. I anxiously followed the enemy's lightning progress on the map . . .

The wireless relentlessly reported the horrifying details of carnage, battles, bombardment, devastation, and civilian massacres. Bulletins were broadcast at mealtimes and one had to get used to eating, drinking, chewing, swallowing, all the while listening to the bloody and disastrous stories in the news. Horror made itself at home in everyday life.

From one day to the next, Paris had fallen strangely silent.

And so began for France that curious military lull, "the Phoney War."

It was then the press initiated an extensive campaign against what was known as "the Fifth Column," which had been growing for years. Keen for a diversion, the general public became obsessed with these sensational revelations.

The prefecture of police instituted "extraordinary measures" of a broad-reaching nature, resolving to conduct a census of all foreigners and to review their status.

These measures, drawn up without any forethought, were implemented on the spot. Police stations, hotel management, landlords, concierges, all those who employed foreigners were asked to ensure compliance with the new regulations.

The whole population started to keep an eye out for "suspects." Overnight, thousands of foreigners took up position in front of the prefecture of police, forming a line that stretched past the Quai aux Fleurs and reached all the way to Boulevard Saint-Michel.

They would start lining up from dawn; they would bring a folding stool, a little food, a book, newspapers, and they would wait, first in the rains of September and October, then through the snow of November and December.

Separated from their countries of origin by the war, with no possibility of return, some without any money or assistance, these people waited, weary and numb. A terrible despondency reigned over this disparate crowd of uprooted souls.

With most able-bodied men having been called up under the general mobilization, the prefecture of police was staffed almost entirely by young women. They were completely unprepared for this enormous task and were quickly overwhelmed.

Armed with my folding stool, I queued for hours on end in order to obtain my residence permit to allow me to remain in France.

It was physically and mentally exhausting. On the inside I was fretting and fuming, but I valiantly endured the official police requirements. All foreigners, regardless of nationality or race, were required to undertake these lengthy formalities, implemented somewhat haphazardly. There was no intent to harass; it was merely a symptom of the general state of disarray.

Thus I waited patiently, some days coughing, and others even suffering a fever.

No matter! It was Paris, Paris with its afternoons spent along the banks of the Seine, next to the *bouquinistes'* stalls, which seemed to have filled with new treasures since my last visit.

The publishers were remarkably generous toward me. They congratulated me and pledged their support for a new bookshop.

The cultural attaché, who had, in turn, arrived back in Paris, had these very encouraging words for me. "You should be credited for remaining at your post until the very last minute." And he added, smiling, "Just like a valiant soldier."

He was trying hard to lessen the pain of separation from my beloved bookshop, just as before he had been so generous in helping me to defend it in the face of every adversity.

And so commenced for me, under a rainy sky, the infinitely dark days of the new war.

At last I obtained my residence permit. It stipulated that I could enjoy France's hospitality until the cessation of hostilities.

◇◇◇

The rhythm of war accelerated at an ever-increasing rate. The Germans breached new borders. The enemy was approaching France. The "Phoney War" was drawing to an end.

However, confident in the strength of the Maginot Line, everybody still considered it impossible that the national border would be crossed.

At that moment, German reconnaissance raids commenced over Paris and its surrounds. Bombs fell on factories in the suburbs.

There was widespread uncertainty. The press and radio lavished us with advice and instructions. The public remained hesitant. Was it better to die in your home or suffocate in a cellar?

When the sirens sounded, some remained in their beds, others went down to the cellar, then came back up or stationed themselves in the stairwell. Some ventured onto the front steps of the building "to see what was going on" and to gossip with neighbors.

Air-raid wardens were strict at first; then they relaxed. "At the end of the day, who knows what's best?" they admitted.

Parisian women took pride in not having been scared and would spend their mornings sharing their experiences on the telephone.

Only when confidence of being able to defend the city fell abruptly, toward the end of May 1940, did people consider abandoning Paris.

The government was advising people to leave; anybody whose presence in the capital was not absolutely necessary should go, and old people should be the first to leave.

Schools closed; the holidays were thus effectively brought forward by two months. Everybody was preparing to leave, and calmly so.

My elderly former professor, who had remained a devoted friend, suggested I follow him to Avignon, where he was heading himself. I remember the two of us sitting there on the terrace of our regular café, La Boule d'Or, on Place Saint-Michel. He was describing to me the delights of the historic town. The Pont d'Avignon, which until then I had known only as the bridge in the song, a memory from the distant past, was to become a reality...

The radio was recommending procuring a safe-conduct pass for the journey, so I took myself off to the police station in my neighborhood very early one morning. I was not in the least astonished to find a line of applicants. After the hours I had spent waiting outside the prefecture of police, I was not about to be put off by anything of that nature.

A group of us were led over to a table where some policemen were sitting. We discovered it would be necessary to get hold of either a medical certificate attesting to the need for a stay at the seaside or in the countryside, or a personal invitation from the place where one was planning to go, preferably from a close relative or, even better, from a patient requiring care.

Some went straight from the police station to besiege doctors' consulting rooms, others discovered relatives of varying degrees of proximity; everybody was just trying to extricate themselves as best they could, and people began to acquire a fresh spirit of innovation to cope with the changing circumstances.

My old friend urgently contacted his godson, who promptly sent me a formal invitation as required.

The appeals to evacuate Paris were growing urgent, but at the same time, safe-conduct passes were increasingly difficult to obtain. I received mine not a moment too soon.

On the eve of my departure from Paris, I received news of my bookshop from the Swedish Ambassador: the boxes of books and records, as well as the furniture and fittings, had been put into storage, thanks to the Swedish Embassy.

Three months later, I was informed by a contact in Switzerland that it had all just been confiscated by order of the German government on the grounds of my race.

Having learned from experience, and in order to guard against all eventualities, I had the notion of asking publishers for a letter of recommendation before I headed off into the unknown. I was directed to the appropriate office of the President of the Council of Ministers where I obtained a document drafted in the following terms:

Madame F*** has for many years been the committed and intelligent manager of a bookshop devoted exclusively to French literature, a bookshop which she established in Berlin in 1921. She has rendered significant service to France through the distribution of French literature abroad. May she avail herself of every freedom and benefit our nation has to offer, the nation for which she has so tirelessly toiled.

The document was signed by a high-ranking official from the office of the President of the Council.

My luggage, two suitcases in total, was swiftly packed; my great trunk, salvaged from Berlin, was put into storage in Paris.

My old friend generously took up position at the Gare de Lyon and, after several hours of waiting, obtained two tickets for Avignon.

Finding a car at that time was a challenge; I stationed myself on the side of the footpath in plenty of time, my two suitcases in front of me, in the hope of snaring a taxi. A good hour later, a driver stopped.

◇◇◇

It was a glorious spring day.

I crossed the city from west to east; the whole Right Bank unfolded before me in a melancholy display, its magnificent perspectives seeming to disappear into infinity.

Paris appeared more beautiful than ever in her imposing grandeur, and as the city passed by I said a painful farewell.

What a fright I had when the driver slowed down a little at Place de la Bastille. An extremely elegant young woman leapt onto the running board of my vehicle and, clinging to the door, said with a charming smile, as if paying a social call, "I hope you don't mind, madame? It's just to reserve the car."

It was so congested in front of the Gare de Lyon that the driver had to set me down at the end of the ramp. I was delighted when a drunkard improvising as a porter offered me his services. Indeed, he acquitted himself of the task admirably.

Half an hour later, we were on our way.

The quiet fields, the peaceful surroundings, the cheerful

countryside unfolding outside, it was still as magnificent as ever. We spoke little. We were thinking about those countries already invaded and ravaged, of the dark night ready to descend over France.

Three days later, Paris was bombed. There were a thousand victims.

War had been unleashed on France. The Germans were approaching the capital.

III

Avignon

My first impression of the capital of the Comtat region was of having been transported back a few centuries in time. I moved into a very old little cottage in a lane that was older still. Despite successive renovations, everything about it harked back to the past: the staircase, the little courtyard, the windows, even the heavy key to my door. At times, I felt as if I were staying with my ancestors.

I would head up onto the city walls, after happily losing myself in a labyrinth of little streets on the way there, and was soon familiar with the views from every angle. A profound silence lent some *quartiers* an unreal atmosphere. Everywhere, it was as if I were in a dream. The city's sleepy peacefulness won me over. I no longer read any newspapers, and I avoided the radio, which was not yet ubiquitous in Avignon.

In the afternoons, crossing the Rhône, I would sit down on one of those great flat slabs of stone on the riverbank, brought there in ancient times, so I'm told, by the town's inhabitants, and remaining their private property. People came here to enjoy the coolness of the river.

I would contemplate the spectacle of the bridge and the Château des Papes, sometimes by day, under the blinding light of the sun, sometimes as dusk smudged the outlines of the old town, turning it into a mirage.

From time to time I would sit in the small public garden. Despite the war, it was maintained, blooming and carefully manicured by the old municipal gardener. Swans glided majestically on the two ponds, children played, carefree; the very elderly would exchange naïve remarks: "Have you read the papers?" "We'll beat them, just like we did in 1918." "They won't try to get all the way down here!" "In Marseille they're saying . . ." "Did you hear on the radio?"

Then, already exhausted from the effort, they would resume their siesta and fall asleep or speak of something else. It was its own little world, that garden, populated by retirees, wealthy *rentiers*, and residents from the old people's home.

One afternoon in the oppressive heat, I was walking down an out-of-the-way little street. I had stopped to admire the pure style of the door and balcony of a house. Around me reigned absolute silence. I stood there, losing all notion of time and place. Suddenly a sweet little window opened slightly and a dear old lady said in a gentle, friendly voice:

"It's very hot today, madame, is it not? Won't you do me the pleasure of accepting a little cider? It's very refreshing!"

Taking her up on this unexpected invitation, I went in. And so

I had the chance to spend an afternoon in a home furnished with the most marvelous antiques. The floor was tiled in exquisite mosaic; the ceiling decorated with cupids, flowers, and crests. The furniture was several centuries old. Portraits of imposing family ancestors stared down at me . . .

As for the cider, it was served to me in a goblet made of silver and gold, a gift from an Avignon pope to one of his noble lords. It was a sacred vessel with the power to protect its owner from the plague that had then been raging through Avignon.

"It will protect you from the enemy," said the aristocratic lady to me, smiling.

I discovered that she knew me by sight and was aware I had fled to her town ahead of the occupying forces.

I took my leave from this kindly hostess late in the day after she had extracted a promise to return.

On my way home, I glimpsed myself in the reflection of a large modern store and felt quite disoriented: all too suddenly, I found myself back in the twentieth century.

My forays into the past could not, however, make me forget the reality of war. Poland, Denmark, Belgium, Holland, all these invaded countries were like pieces of the planet that had been wrenched off, with no hope of contact, and only infrequent and distant signs of devastation and suffering were still making their way through to us.

My despair for my family knew no bounds; I could see no end to it.

France, too, was bleeding. Even though people tried to recall the years of 1914–1918 and readily conjured up memories of the Marne, present times defied any comparison. All one could see was a world collapsing.

IV

Vichy

V ery quickly, distressing anxiety took hold of me again.
I lost all contact with the past and again found myself
abruptly facing the full horror of reality, the reality of war.

When my cousins, who had fled from Belgium, announced
that they had just arrived in Vichy and suggested I join them, I
felt a real hunger to see these members of my family again.

My kindly professor, as always full of sage advice, discouraged
me from setting out; he advised me to trust to Fate and to wait,
calmly, on the banks of the Rhône, for events to unfold.

While acknowledging the wisdom of his counsel, I could no
longer stay put. I needed a change of scene, too, and I was drawn
to the mere idea of a move.

I sent my two suitcases ahead and took the train for Vichy. It took twenty hours to reach Clermont-Ferrand, going through Nîmes.

Along the way, as we followed the river Allier, which seemed to be accompanying us, I gazed in wonder at the Cévennes Mountains, with their bewitching golden carpets of broom flowers.

The train stopped frequently, and passengers would get off to stretch their legs; they bought bread, cheese, and fruit from the local farmers. A sense of congenial camaraderie hung in the air. It felt like an escape from more serious concerns.

Soldiers joined us everywhere along the way. Most of them were heading to Clermont-Ferrand, others were returning home; large numbers were making their way to their designated mustering stations.

I remember an officer, entering our compartment, saying: "No point going any further, you poor sods! You're better off turning around and heading back to where you've come from. There's fighting at Moulins! The Germans have occupied most of France."

Nobody took his pronouncements seriously. We knew the Germans had reached Paris on the fourteenth of June! How could they have crossed the whole of the north of France and made it across the Loire in just a few days?

But once we arrived in Clermont-Ferrand, we discovered that German troops were indeed making their way up the river Allier. There was widespread panic!

I had no choice but to join my cousins as quickly as possible. I departed for Vichy on a train that had been scheduled out of timetable for the few passengers present. Already, all regular connections had been interrupted.

It was around six o'clock in the morning when I arrived at my destination. I made my way to their house and from a distance

I could see my cousin busy attaching a mattress to his car with ropes. Next to him were several bundles. Seeing me, he lifted his arms heavenwards:

"You poor woman! What are you doing here in Vichy? We sent you a telegram telling you to forget any idea of travel!"

I replied, "That's possible, but nothing ever reached me."

Such was my arrival in Vichy.

After embracing my cousins, I set about preparing for our departure, along with everybody else. At ten o'clock we took our position in the queue of cars heading for Clermont-Ferrand.

Out on the highway, cars were moving four abreast. Everywhere there were trucks laden with women, children, and the elderly. Perched on chairs, the old people were balancing a child, a cat, a dog, a cage, baskets, or loaves of bread on their laps. Next to them, livestock and rabbits.

As far as the eye could see, cyclists were hemmed in by more trucks, horse-drawn vehicles, and cars covered in mattresses.

In front of us was a car with its back window broken. Every second moment, an old lady would anxiously call through the hole to ask, "Are my animals still there?" On the luggage rack was a box with rabbits, a cat in a basket, and canaries in a cage. We reassured the dear woman.

The line of cars was advancing at a rate of a kilometer every hour. From time to time we would get out and walk along the side of the road. And when we did, we could see the stream of evacuees disappearing into the distance.

At one point, soldiers appeared from the opposite direction. As the road was completely blocked, they were making their way as best they could through the fields. They shouted out to us, "We're heading for Moulins . . . they're fighting there. There's no point pushing on to Clermont-Ferrand, you lot. Not only is there nowhere to stay and nothing to eat, even the water supply is starting to run out . . . As for petrol, not a drop!"

They seemed jaded. Many of them were walking in old slippers and carrying their boots tied by a string from their shoulder.

Further on, heading up fifty-odd artillerymen who were just as weary as the infantrymen preceding them, we came across several trucks, on top of which were perched French 75 guns! The refugees' vehicles had to pull over onto the shoulders to make room for them.

The troop movement must have been spotted by German reconnaissance planes. Shortly afterward, a clamor broke out: "Airplanes, airplanes!" The Clermont-Ferrand anti-aircraft guns fired. A few German bombs fell. People dashed pell-mell for the ditches.

Once the line of people started to move again, my cousin decided, "If Clermont-Ferrand is packed to the rafters with people fleeing, it makes more sense to return to Vichy, especially as I wouldn't have enough petrol to get back from Clermont."

We agreed and, at the first turnoff, he put his foot down and headed back to Vichy. We were very surprised to see the number of other evacuees who followed us.

We returned to a silent and mournful Vichy.

We expected the Germans to arrive at any moment.

The advance scouts of the invasion had made it as far as the town hall.

◇◇◇

The first to arrive at six o'clock in the evening were numerous motorcycles, followed shortly afterward by artillery, tanks, cavalry, and foot soldiers, then a multitude of trucks.

The occupation of Vichy was under way. That evening, the whole town was talking about the thousands of baths the Germans had ordered, not only in hotels but even at the thermal spring establishment, not to mention the innumerable bottles of champagne consumed.

The occupying forces left the town's administration in the hands of the French authorities for the time being. They had other matters to attend to.

Numerous covered trucks passed through the town heading for unknown destinations. When they lifted their tarpaulins to load fresh booty, one could see the provisions piled high inside.

One day, a crowd of eager children had gathered around one such truck. I saw that the vehicle had been filled with blocks of Menier chocolate.

The trucks would frequently pull up in front of the abattoir and people would watch the Germans carry off entire freshly slaughtered carcasses. Then the housewives would take up their position in line at the butchers in order to buy a thin slice of meat.

That was still the Golden Age, though: meat every day, and up to seventy-five grams at a time.

The population of Vichy were still going about their daily lives. People were happy merely to avoid the occupying forces. One stayed away from the cafés they frequented. People left shops, abandoning their shopping on the counter, if one of them came through the door.

The Germans enjoyed buying stockings, but not, on any account, they would say, "artificial silk." In the confectioners' they would eat cakes and ice creams by the dozen and would exclaim, thinking nobody could understand them: "And to think it only costs four *pfennigs* each! Isn't it a scream!"

While the privates would buy anything they could lay their hands on in the shops, the officers, sparkling in their immaculate uniforms, would fill the seats on the terraces of the grand ice-cream cafés, downing bottles of champagne from morning onward.

The occupiers had not yet acquired the "art of consumption."

Locals, refugees, demobilized soldiers, they all went past in the streets, observing this strange spectacle. Everybody grew increasingly irritable with every day that passed, complaining about everyone and everything: about daily hardships, difficulties in getting in supplies, the hard times, the bleak future, the daily spectacle of the enemy, the country's leaders, and the abyss into which we had all been plunged.

Bitterness filled the hearts of the French.

A bitterness that was to rise like the tide across Occupied France.

◇◇◇

The handsome post office, the pride and joy of Vichy locals, kept its doors and windows obstinately shut. Every day, crowds walked past, "just to check."

How great the joy, then, when at last the post office reopened and one could send first cards, then letters. People would write sitting down, standing up, at the counters, outside the post office, sitting on benches. People were writing everywhere, and everybody was writing. People who had never enjoyed holding a pen were sending cards in these lonely times; everybody was feeling the need for family, friends, for human relationships.

With correspondence attended to, then came the impatient wait for replies. From morning to evening, there would be fifty to eighty people stationed in front of the two counters open for that purpose.

An old gentleman with a handsome head of white hair, who was my neighbor from the bench in the park, would take up his position in line every day too, leaning on his cane, and each time he would go away empty-handed. I put his disappointment down to the slowness of the postal system.

"Still nothing?" I said to him one day, as we left the post office together.

"The truth of the matter is, I'm not waiting for letters. But time passes more quickly at the post office, in the company of others, and standing in front of the counter, well, that in itself is enough to make one feel a little hopeful," he replied, in all seriousness.

One day, a lad of about ten years lined up. He duly waited his turn.

"Poor little thing," said the lady ahead of me over her shoulder (for there would be many a good chat had in the queue), "he has probably been torn away from his family."

When it came his turn at the counter, the boy asked the clerk for a strip of sticky tape. He was sharply rebuked. The exodus had brought him to Vichy, and while waiting to be reunited with his family, he was playing "postman" with some other youngsters and he absolutely had to have sticky tape for the stamps in this game of make-believe.

An old lady came to bring back to the counter a letter she had opened but which was not addressed to her. The clerk asked:

"Aren't you Madame Guilloux, then?"

"Yes."

"Madeleine?"

"No, Marie."

"Why did you take the letter?"

"You handed it to me, sir, and the sender might have made a mistake."

"What? Your own family, make a mistake? Don't they know your first name?" said the clerk, severely.

"You know, it's easy to lose track of things in these times of war."

"True enough," said the clerk in a conciliatory tone.

The post office clerk, moreover, was delighted with his job. For a letter received, a cigarette would be discreetly left as a sign of gratitude, accompanied by a complicit smile or an emotional "*Merci.*" Sometimes, however, he had nothing to give but explanations. "Why isn't such-and-such a letter here yet?"—"It's odd it has taken so long to arrive!"—"It's the war," came his invariable reply, patient and philosophical.

The post office served not only as the major means of contact with the world—the miraculous invention that channeled the voice of somebody who had disappeared, an appeal, a response—it also served to fill the overwhelming hours of emptiness. It replaced the solitude with vague hope and created a form of human solidarity among those gathered at the counter. People would speak to each other as they left or greet each other in the street with a "*Bonjour.*"

The loneliness of those weeks was a dreadful burden evident on faces at the station, at the post office, on park benches, on café terraces, everywhere.

◇◇◇

I had decided to return immediately to Avignon by train. But the day after the Occupation, the doors to the railway station were closed and a sign announced the suspension of regular trains until further notice.

Thus began a daily pilgrimage to the station.

The fateful sign remained in place for days on end. Looking through the grille, one could see trains, but each time the hope of being able to take one was met with disappointment: they were all trains that had been commandeered for use by the Germans or as food supply convoys.

During that time of military occupation, I was fortunate to find a room boarding with railway workers, right on the edge of town. It was a sweet little cottage, surrounded by flowers, the result of two generations of workers' savings; but a magnificent municipal abattoir had subsequently been erected immediately opposite. When the wind blew toward the house, it carried with it the acrid smell of blood. The mournful bellowing of the beasts could be heard day and night. The proximity of such neighbors weighed on me strangely.

With the armistice signed, my cousins had returned to Belgium.

I had stayed, alone, separated from my family, from my friends, lost in an abyss of melancholy.

The two suitcases I had sent from Avignon arrived just as I was contemplating leaving. I had grown accustomed to the most primitive habits in the last six weeks. And so the clothes that arrived felt superfluous.

At last regular trains for the general public resumed.

One cannot begin to imagine the scene of my departure from Vichy!

As soon as the first train was announced—in fact, it turned out to be made up of goods wagons—thousands of people prepared to leave. First the refugees, whom fate had abandoned there in their flight, those who had come to the springs for their cure and whom the war had surprised in Vichy, demobilized soldiers, among them the injured, all of whom had been held up there for weeks, they all wished to leave. Many Vichy locals were also hoping to seek refuge with relatives or friends, in order to get out of the Occupied Zone.

Those wishing to travel crowded outside and around the railway station, as well as on the embankment along the tracks.

Red Cross refreshment stalls had opened up here and there, offering coffee, bread, cheese, and fruit.

Refugees and soldiers sat eating on the ground, their food spread out simply on newspapers. At night, their knapsacks served as pillows.

Whenever a train was announced, people would rouse themselves into action; sometimes, as it pulled into the station, the engine would have to slow down to allow the crowd time to clear the tracks. The stationmaster would shout and gesticulate, waving his flag, ringing a bell. People would respond: "All right, all right . . . We're moving . . . we're moving! My, how that stationmaster carries on! We've been waiting long enough for the train!"

And so trains arrived with no prior warning, bringing demobilized and injured French soldiers, as well as occupying troops, to Vichy.

When a train did stop, and the possibility of securing a place presented itself, there was a great crush to get on! In just a few minutes, every compartment, the corridors, and even the roofs of the carriages would be invaded. Veritable clusters of humans would hang from the running boards . . . People climbed through the windows. Those who hadn't been able to find a place were forced to wait anew, for hours, days even. They would return to where they had been camping out and resume their games of cards. "Oh well," they'd say, philosophically, "we've waited six weeks, we'll wait another day or two."

Everybody was worn out, apathetic.

I received kindly letters from my old professor, urging me to return to Avignon.

One day, flanked by my two suitcases, it was my turn to take up position on the platform. One case served as a seat, on the other I set out my provisions and a book.

I will never forget the train coming into the station and the journey that followed. It comprised about fifteen wagons: at the head of the train, five passenger cars, then ten open goods wagons, their floors strewn with straw.

The refugees rushed forward, as usual, and it was a matter of seeing who, be it the weakest or the strongest, would prevail in that struggle.

The train was already packed when the doors of the waiting room opened: the wounded, carried on stretchers, on chairs, or supporting each other, moved onto the platform.

The stationmaster shouted: "Make some space for the wounded!"

Every able-bodied man stood and got off. The injured were settled in compartments, stretched out on the banquettes or seated. Some of them, those more seriously injured, were laid out on the straw of the goods wagons, where they were more comfortable.

Nurses announced that there were still a few places available for the elderly and for women and children. There was one for me. Those still able to climb in made do and settled wherever they could. We were cramped, but happy.

At last the train set off. If the truth be told, it was only moving at a walking pace. At the next station, a new crush of passengers! This time, all the corridors were stormed. Some soldiers had perched atop the luggage racks. Protestations rang out: "Make room for passengers, not luggage! Leave it at the next station!"

We found ourselves queuing up at the door of the left luggage office at some small, unknown station. Whoever had bags left them there with a request to send them on after us—but not without some apprehension: their future seemed rather uncertain . . .

The train stopped continuously for mysterious reasons that nobody even tried to divine. We took advantage of the stops to stretch our legs, after begging those who were not getting up to save our places.

Notwithstanding the slowness of the journey and our discomfort, time did not seem to drag.

Looking out the windows, soldiers spoke of the land to which they were returning.

One said, anxiously: "I wonder, how have they managed back home? There weren't enough hands even before we left!"

"It seems they're making do regardless," replied another. "As long as it's a good harvest."

"It looks as if it's been dry through these parts," objected a third.

He gestured to the vast open spaces before him with a sweep of his hand.

"Yes," sighed the first, dreamily, "they seem to be making do."

He pulled a photograph out of his pocket.

"Look, this is my eldest. He's already a man, and no layabout, not in the field nor at the dinner table! This here's my missus, she's nearly fifty, though you wouldn't know it!"

"No, you wouldn't know it," replied the other.

And he, in turn, showed a photo of his Louise. Quite a looker, they thought, but were careful not to overdo it. She was his betrothed, and it wouldn't do to joke about it. That was sacred territory . . .

One soldier pulled out a bag wrapped in newsprint. He wanted to give it to his wife. Presents chosen hastily, a quarter of an hour before running for the train, were passed from hand to hand.

Among them, a small doll brought back by a beardless recruit for his six-year-old sister.

"I saw it in Vichy and thought I'd buy it because it looks so much like my little sister it could be her twin."

Everybody laughed.

Nobody spoke of war, nor of the future.

The joking around, the storytelling, the coarse language that once upon a time would have rung out in third-class carriages had disappeared.

Nor was there any talk of the dark days.

But the weight of those days could be felt in the rough-hewn hearts of those soldiers, in the decency of their remarks, in their looks that followed fields and meadows to the slow rhythm of the train.

◇◇◇

We'd often cross paths with other trains; then there'd be conversations, an exchange of news, and even some extraordinarily fortunate chance meetings.

Nuns, Red Cross nurses, and country folk would come to distribute provisions, drinks, and newspapers, along with words of encouragement.

The train would slowly resume its journey. Soldiers would open their kit bags and pull out bread and cheese, handing around their flasks of wine. They drank without allowing their lips to touch the bottle.

There was a sense of solidarity among all the passengers as they faced their uncertain futures. Everybody got along, avoided arguments, shared their supplies, breathed as one. Someone gave me a hearty hunk of cheese with a slice of brown bread.

My neighbor, almost a child, a young blond lad who had been wounded, offered me a piece of chocolate. During the night, his bent leg was giving him so much pain that he stretched it over my knees in his sleep, and I sat without moving so as not to wake him.

I can no longer recall if the journey lasted eighteen or twenty-four hours. Once we arrived in Avignon, we all had to spend the night on the waiting-room benches: the town was so overcrowded that the police did not allow us to leave the station before daybreak. Only the injured were taken to the hospitals.

The following day, I went to meet my dear professor in the peaceful public garden. I found him sitting in the sun, as if I had left only the day before. He greeted me with his customary kindliness and complimented me on how well I looked, teasing me about my odyssey to Vichy.

I was forced to recount every eventful moment.

As I told my story, I grew acutely aware that the journey, while ultimately pointless, had not been a total loss. I had lived among the French locals, and witnessed their persistent cheerfulness and sense of perspective even in the face of misfortune.

I was a little sorry about my suitcases, which had not yet reappeared, despite the resumption of trains. Three weeks later, however, after much meandering, they faithfully returned to me in Avignon, just as they had in Vichy. But in what a state! Lids dented, straps torn off, padlocks rusted. True casualties of war! Inside, my clothes were covered in mildew. But nothing, not a single thing, was missing.

This time, the clerk at the left luggage office was ready with an apt remark:

"Hundreds of trunks have gone missing," he said, "you're in luck!"

Had not the clerk at the Gare du Nord made much the same comment upon the arrival of my trunk in Paris? Yet now that trunk, which had so miraculously survived, had been confiscated by the Germans in Paris on the grounds of my race. I had just learned as much from a postcard sent to me in Avignon by the storage depot.

V

Avignon

August–November 1940

How the atmosphere of a town can change in a few weeks!
When I had left Avignon in June, peaceful Provence
still exuded its charm. The elderly dozed in sweet bliss in the
public garden among children playing around the ornamental
lakes. At mealtimes, the tempting smell of dishes heavily fla-
vored with garlic would waft from restaurants. Beautiful girls
walked the streets in the afternoons, playful and in love. Boys
would smile at them and toss gallantries their way. There were
peaceful people all around. Life in the town continued its calm,
trouble-free existence, a world away from the war.

Now the benches were occupied by soldiers, some with
bandaged legs and arms. The wounded sat at the windows and

on the balconies of several hotels that had been turned into hospitals, getting some fresh air. German officers and soldiers strutted through the streets. You could hear the metallic chatter of typewriters from hotel windows. The so-called "economic commission" was creating unrest in that peaceful medieval city.

In June, the market had been spilling over with slabs of butter, mounds of fruit, the most diverse array of cheeses, and beautiful fresh meat on the butchers' blocks.

Now, there was no butter to be found, nor any cheese. The good humor and chitter-chatter of housewives had vanished.

A queuing system had been instituted outside shops and at the market. A morose silence reigned, interrupted from time to time by quarreling and arguments.

Demobilized French soldiers from all branches of the military waited for trains that would take them back to their homes. Every day there were departures. Those from occupied parts of the country received instructions indicating which convoys they were to take in alphabetical order. Those from the "forbidden zones" had no choice but to give up any hope of return. They were assigned temporary places to stay. Instructions were posted at the town hall and in the newspapers, and broadcast on the radio.

Demoralized and at a loose end, they lingered on café terraces, on benches, in the bright sunshine in front of the Palais des Papes. They detested talking about the war. They seemed to know nothing of events in which they had participated!

When pressed further, they replied: "It seems the war is over. We were told to leave and we left, and we haven't arrived anywhere. There you have it! It's all a bit odd, but what do you want us to say? You've got your newspapers, all you've got to do is read them." And then one of them, pointing to the radio, said: "There you go! He knows more about it than we do and he's much more of a talker! Ah! The bastards! I wish someone would shut them up! They've put us in a right mess!"

One day, very early, I went to sit in the public garden to take in the cool morning air. A woman came and sat next to me. In her hands she held a missal and her rosary. She greeted me with a few words, as was the custom in this part of the world; then, soon enough, she started to tell me her story.

She had come from Château-Renard to see her son who was receiving treatment in the hospital, in the "shell shock" ward. Artillery bombardments had shattered his nerves. He recognized his mother, but did not seem to be himself: he was talking about the bombs, the blood, the friends he had seen collapsing next to him, not making much sense, and was clearly reliving those dramatic events again and again. She was allowed to visit him for two hours, morning and evening. So, just as you would with a small child, she would speak to him about home, about his brothers and sisters, about his school friends and the farm animals, thus trying to rekindle his interest in all the things it seemed his mind had erased.

I saw this mother on two more occasions. She told me about the improvements she thought she could notice.

One morning, I ran into her guiding a young soldier in hospital pajamas by the arm. She was glowing . . .

They passed by; I would never see them again.

At that time, the police in Avignon started to "organize" the refugees. We were all summoned to the town hall, and once again, we had to line up, this time under a scorching sun.

Turning our papers this way and that, the gendarmes of this

tranquil city consulted each other; they seemed so uncomfortable one felt sorry for them. They examined circulars and regulations, haphazardly issuing information, orders, and instructions.

After examining my passport, one of them asked me in an interrogating tone:

"An ally? You *are* an ally, aren't you? Yes, that's obvious enough, isn't it? Ah! Yes, the Polish! Now they're what you call strapping fellows. They fought hard! Yes, that's all right, then!"

Of course, I agreed with everything he said and . . . my residence permit was vigorously stamped with the seal of the municipality.

Those were the days!

This time, my stay in Avignon was to last from August to the end of November.

I went often to the municipal library; I was curious about the life and works of Frédéric Mistral. Seated next to me, my professor was studying the same author in the original Provençal text, delighted to be able to read it fluently. The library contained the most complete collection of documents relating to the history of Avignon.

In the afternoons, I would go to sit on the banks of the Rhône and spend hours watching the strong current of the river. It dragged along the most varied of objects, even trees it appeared to have uprooted in its enthusiasm. Sometimes, you could see a tree tossed about like a wisp of straw in its swirling eddies, sometimes you saw it drawn up to its full height, innumerable drops of water hanging from its leaves, glittering like diamonds in the sun.

As autumn approached, the Rhône started to rise before one's very eyes. It covered the embankments, submerging plants and small trees, swamped the riverside, and climbed all the way up the pylons of bridges.

The weather in Avignon grew ever colder. At night, the wind beat furiously against windows and shutters, rattling houses and shaking trees with titanic force.

It violently attacked anybody who was out and about.

I experienced the true force of the mistral wind one day when it blew me a good stretch down the road and threw me against a tree, which was shaking from top to bottom.

My dear professor, such a calm fellow, had also fallen victim to the wind, and announced that he was simply going to flee the mistral and head for Nice, his favorite winter retreat.

◇◇◇

There was nothing to keep me in Avignon. There was no news from my relatives, not a single sign of life. I was pining and anxious, and it made me long for a change of scene.

A safe-conduct pass was required in order to travel to Nice. The visa office had been set up in a gracious little palace, the former residence of a cardinal. Its courtyard was shaded by plane trees. A fountain murmured at its center. As I waited, I admired the windows and doors, decorated with the most beautiful wrought-iron designs.

When it came my turn to appear before the gendarme responsible, I almost regretted having to leave my spot.

"Are you a foreigner?" asked the gendarme in a strong local accent. And he added, "No visas to Nice for foreigners, my dear lady. Nothing to be done!"

That afternoon, my professor, accompanied by his godson, Monsieur Olive, found me on the terrace of our usual café.

I told him of my disappointment that morning and exclaimed, half seriously, half jesting:

"If only I could find a Frenchman for a marriage of convenience so I can be free of these eternal trials and tribulations!"

"The problem is, France is harboring too many foreigners," remarked Monsieur Olive, sententiously.

We spoke of other matters.

The following day, at around five o'clock, we found ourselves back on the terrace of the same café. Monsieur Olive appeared, beaming. He was gesturing to us from afar and, nearing us, he whispered:

"I have him, I have him . . . your future husband! He'll be here in a moment."

He swiftly explained the situation and told us what to do:

"You, madame, you'll sit off to one side a little, so as not to get involved in the initial discussion. We'll take a seat inside."

In broken sentences, he told us he had discovered a fellow who was prepared to "go through with it" and whom he had told to come at a quarter past five.

"And here he is, what do you know!" he cried.

Then, hurrying to the door:

"Over here, my dear friend, over here!"

We saw a little old man of about seventy scurry over, neat and tidy, leaning on a cane and doffing his straw hat. Monsieur Olive took care of the introductions.

"Monsieur Devitrolles, retired shopkeeper, currently resident in the old people's home in town—my godfather."

From my corner, I was able to witness the conversation as a mute spectator.

"Well then, Monsieur Devitrolles," started Monsieur Olive,

"as I've explained to you, you're going to marry a lady who needs your good name. You'll receive a certain sum, allowing you to improve your everyday fare at the old people's home. And on top of that, you'll get a fine suit, a black hat, and a tie to wear to the town hall. But immediately after the wedding, your wife will leave . . . you've understood, that's all settled?"

"Understood," replied the old gentleman, "but I have to *see* her, this lady." (He pronounced the word "see" with the twang of the Provençal accent.)

"Of course you'll see her," replied Monsieur Olive, "but this lady, a foreigner, she's going to leave the very evening of the wedding."

"A foreigner?" inquired Monsieur Devitrolles, interested. "She's not from the Auvergne, though, is she, this foreigner? It's just that I'm not at all fond of people from the Auvergne."

"No, she's not from the Auvergne, not at all, but it hardly matters, for in any event she's leaving again. You understand?"

"She's in quite a hurry, this lady, my wife," observed Monsieur Devitrolles.

"Yes, she's in a hurry . . . she's leaving for America!"

"*Oh la, la, la, la*, she's not doing things by halves. The Americas! That's a long way away."

"Yes, it's a long way away," answered the tireless Monsieur Olive, "but she's leaving, and there you'll be, right back to your old ways. All right, then?"

"All right by me, but I have to *see* her, this woman."

"Yes, yes, you'll see her. You'll get a good enough glimpse of her," replied Monsieur Olive, showing a little humor; "you'll get a good enough glimpse. Anyway, she's heading for eighty and she's slightly hunchbacked." (With these fabricated details, Monsieur

Olive was hoping to discourage Monsieur Devitrolles once and for all, who seemed not to have understood that it was to be a mere marriage of convenience.)

Monsieur Devitrolles's response was categorical and unexpected:

"Well, that doesn't suit me at all! We hardly want an eighty-year-old hunchback, now, do we! Oh no! I'm having none of that!"

"But I'm telling you, she's leaving! She's leaving! She's leaving! How many times do I have to repeat it!" Monsieur Olive was shouting now.

"I'm not having any of your hunchback," said Monsieur Devitrolles, with finality, and he too was furious now, rapping his cane on the marble tabletop.

My dear professor, unable to take any more, let out a peal of Homeric laughter. I was chuckling behind my newspaper. The scene was becoming more and more ridiculous.

Other customers were starting to look over. Monsieur Olive had lost his patience.

"You're nothing but an old fool," he shouted.

Monsieur Devitrolles stood up—but not before downing the remains of his Chambéry-fraise aperitif—retrieved his cane and his hat, and left, dignified and grumbling.

Monsieur Olive looked at us as if calling us to witness.

"It's no laughing matter," he said, truly irritated. "I'd tracked down a serious contender, nothing compromising, a permanent resident of an old people's home with an aristocratic name to top it all off, and *voilà*, we can't even get things off the ground. I picked a crazy, just my luck."

The poor boy dabbed at his brow. Then, having calmed down, it was his turn to laugh.

My professor and I had enjoyed the comedy of this interlude, so symptomatic of the times.

There were a fair few marriages of convenience in France in those days. These absurd ploys allowed one to evade complications for a certain period. Sometime around 1942, however, these marriages were annulled.

VI

Nice

December 1940

S ome French friends sent me an invitation stamped by the prefecture in Nice that helped considerably: I immediately obtained the precious safe-conduct pass.

I left Avignon in midwinter, leaving behind me cold, wind, and rain. From Marseille, it felt as if I were moving through an enchanted land. The Corniche was golden with mimosas and fields of carnations: everywhere lemon, orange, and olive trees, their branches laden with fruit, stood out against the background of dark-green palms. An azure-blue sea and sky framed the exotic world spread out before me.

I felt as if I had been transported to a land of fairy tales. I was dazzled. I was entering an earthly paradise!

Little did I know that, at the same time, I was heading into the darkest period of my life!

A friend of mine from Paris was waiting for me at the railway station in Nice. As she led me to Rue de France, where we boarded an old-fashioned little tram that coughed along with a great metallic clatter, she filled me in on life in Nice. She took me to a small hotel at the beach, in the Sainte-Hélène neighborhood.

Every window of the hotel, which was surrounded by palms and lemon trees, had a view of the sea's vast horizon.

A few days later, I made contact with some people from Paris who I knew had taken refuge in Nice.

At first, there were the distressing revelations about all that had happened in the capital: the bombing of Auteuil, the Occupation, the mass exodus!

I also heard terrible news about the countries that had been occupied and, once again, I was overcome by heartrending anxiety for my family.

Information arrived by way of the few foreign newspapers one could still find at the time. Of those, the Zurich weekly *Die Weltwoche* was enormously popular.

Other news spread by word of mouth, crossing borders, defying censorship and monitoring, reaching us fresh and leaving us breathless with horror. At that time, there was scarcely anything but disastrous news.

I also discovered no end of detail about local life, its possibilities and its challenges: the greatest difficulty was obtaining a residence permit . . . People were being rejected in their hundreds.

A week or so later, armed with information and advice, I went to the prefecture.

I came via Quai des États-Unis and Rue Saint-François-de-

Paule, and found myself suddenly in the midst of a splendid garden of cut flowers.

It was the day of the flower market! Delighted, I gazed at the whole display, then I stopped in front of the stalls to take a closer look. Carnations of every possible variety dominated at that time of year. In 1940, there was still fruit available, which added to the scene. (After that, oranges, lemons, and mandarins were only to be seen on trees; once requisitioned, they would disappear from the market and from shop windows.)

Time was getting on. I hurried on to the prefecture. As I drew closer, I saw a long unmoving queue of people. It extended around the corner of the official building.

Policemen paced up and down.

I felt suddenly faint and hesitated a moment. But there was no putting it off!

I took my position in the queue.

It was two o'clock in the afternoon. At about five o'clock, I found myself at the counter. For the first time, it occurred to me to resort to my letter of recommendation from the office of the President of the Council of Ministers. I proffered my papers to the clerk. He glanced over them rapidly:

"Office of the President of the Council! Prime Minister Daladier! None of that means anything anymore!"

Refused.

But I seemed to have one definite stroke of good fortune amid my administrative difficulties. Twenty-four hours prior to my scheduled forced departure from Nice, the two local newspapers reported that hotels, suffering terribly due to the war, had protested against the deportation orders. The hotel industry, on the brink of collapse, was seeking residency permits on behalf of foreigners. It was agreeing to do its part to work with suppliers to ensure there would be sufficient food.

Thus, due to a combination of unforeseen circumstances, I was able to remain in Nice.

I liked my small hotel and I decided to stay put. A restful silence reigned all day long, complemented by the murmur of the sea.

But at mealtimes, the sound of raised voices rang out through the building. Monsieur Thérive, the hotel's manager and head chef, a garrulous, self-confident man of insipid good looks, was fiendishly obsessed with politics. From hors d'oeuvres through to coffee, he had the radio turned up so loudly that he was providing a news service to his neighbors, not to mention to passersby.

And it was precisely the radio that supplied him with the topics for the polemics he threw himself into so wholeheartedly. As a general rule, discussion would take place between radio broadcasts, but when matters heated up, the announcer's voice could no longer keep them quiet.

The hotel's owner, Madame Marguerite, a small, retiring person, gentle-natured and utterly unpretentious, would then discreetly turn the volume knob down. Often those arguing would not even notice.

The chef was an avowed enemy of the Germans and an anti-Semite "on principle."

Monsieur Martin, a demobilized naval officer and a very handsome man, would fly into a white rage every time a comment was made in favor of the British. He would often remove himself mid-meal so as not to have to listen to any such praise.

Monsieur Petitjean, a tall, sporty student who ran a youth

camp in Nice, was a staunch collaborationist. He deferred, in all matters, to the Germans, "the most sensible people on Earth," he said. Reveling in its anti-Semitic diatribes, he would refer his dinner companions to *Mein Kampf*, a translated copy of which he owned and would happily lend.

Monsieur Huyard, a retired colonel from the First World War, argued against these excessive notions, "which," he said, "would lead to the downfall of France, a balanced, moderate, and tolerant country."

As for the refugees, they did not participate in discussions. Offended by these indirect attacks, they would confer with each other about the possibility of a change of hotel and atmosphere; but politics was being discussed everywhere, and equally vehemently.

When they thought of the persecution rife in so many other countries, their own lives seemed almost enviable, and they would fall silent.

Pride was no longer appropriate. It was an inaccessible luxury, even for the French at that time.

Fortunately, after people had eaten, the hotel would fall back into its usual, soothing silence.

◇◇◇

One day, Monsieur Thérive announced that it would make his job much easier if hotel residents would eat in town from now on. It was becoming impossible to get in enough supplies.

From then on, I ate lunch and dinner at various different restaurants.

I grew to know Nice's old quarters, the picturesque language of its population, and the very particular cuisine of the Midi.

The Promenade des Anglais was depressingly banal, with its great buildings that looked like private hospitals butting up against exaggeratedly modernist apartment blocks, its kiosks and its rustic buildings. The artificial atmosphere of most of the cafés and other public places was painful, almost palpably sad.

The rich went to inhale the ambiance of the casino, losing enormous sums without even being true gamblers. I recall one Viennese woman saying to her husband in a bewildered voice:

"My poor darling, what came over you, when you've always had such a horror of gambling?"

"I gamble so I can forget; I'm more horrified by my own thoughts than I am by the gambling."

In order to kill time, some people went on excursions out of town and returned, exhausted.

In villas and in hotels, entire days were devoted to bridge, with people playing mindlessly late into the night.

Others preferred to stay at home or to go to a friend's to talk politics. Pointless discussions, for nobody managed to resolve anything.

A large number of refugees were preparing to emigrate. They were relying on relatives, some more distant than others, on friends or the friends of friends, on acquaintances who had settled in far-off corners of the world, who they believed would help them.

They engaged in painstaking, carefully worded correspondence and sent costly telegrams asking for affidavits and visas, only to receive replies, queries, questionnaires, and circulars back in response which would prompt a whole new wave of correspondence.

Then, they would spend entire mornings waiting at consulates only to discover this or that document was missing, did not comply with regulations, or had turned out to be incorrect. When some did emerge with a visa it seemed a phenomenal feat, and they the blessed ones!

Departures were few.

Emigration offices and agencies offered to provide information and take care of formalities while making grand promises of success. They took down payments and deposits, paid eagerly by the refugees. But the promises never came to anything. The emigrants thought they'd been robbed; at least they'd had a period of hope.

My affections and my ties held me in Europe and I made no attempt to emigrate.

Everybody had lost their drive, their enthusiasm for life . . . And so, from time to time, we would fall into gloomy indifference, an all-consuming inertia.

When I felt like seeing people, I had only to head to the Promenade des Anglais. I just had to take a seat somewhere around Boulevard Gambetta, the casino, or the Jardin Albert-Premier in order to run into "acquaintances," whose names one would often not even remember, or to meet new ones. These lost souls, far from family and friends, were keen to break the all-too-heavy silence, either to ease their minds by sharing their worries, or just to have a chat and hear the latest news of political events or the stories of other refugees. Anything was better than to languish in isolation.

One day, a seventy-two-year-old Polish woman told me the story of her flight, in the course of which she had lost her entire family. She had half lost her mind, too.

Similarly, I also met a Norwegian woman sitting on a bench,

whose husband had escaped just as he had been about to be arrested and taken hostage as an act of reprisal. She had rejoined him in Sweden, then they had come ... to Nice! Now they were considering heading for England, where he wanted to enlist. She was following him wherever he went.

A Dutch millionaire was waiting for help from friends in America: he had run out of funds.

An elderly couple, diamond merchants, one hundred and fifty years old between them, had left Antwerp with precious stones sewn into the lining of their clothes and were complaining to all and sundry about the great fortune they had lost. English people and Americans staying in the luxury hotels continued to stroll the promenades and make day trips until such time as their respective governments ordered them to get on the first boat out.

People from every country, separated from their families and alone, would linger outside the casino, in front of shop windows, on streets and in squares, anywhere. They occupied benches and chairs, filling cafés and their terraces from morning to evening.

Jews from all the occupied countries wandered around, disoriented, purposeless, and without hope, in an ever-increasing state of anxiety and agitation.

It was the lack of anything to do that weighed most heavily, draining every ounce of energy, any resistance.

One morning I sat down looking out to sea next to an unusually beautiful young lady with distinctly Slavic features. She was knitting. After a few minutes, she engaged me in conversation. Having cast a furtive glance around us, she turned to face me and confided, almost whispering in my ear, that she was knitting to bring in some money. She asked if I would recommend her services occasionally, begging me at the same time not to betray her confidence, as if her work constituted a crime! And it was, too. I was about to find out as much to my own detriment.

I had discovered an old book dealer on Rue Gioffredo. We chatted amid the secondhand volumes in his shop. The fellow was more interested in his business than in his profession. He spoke of remittances, profits, stationery, customers, the difficult times we were living in. I was examining his dusty volumes as I listened to him, and observed he had some rare titles. I told him I would like to catalogue his books. Seeing his hesitation, I added that, of course, I would do the work for free, out of my own love of books. He eagerly agreed. Armed with a letter he had drafted, I took myself off to the relevant department to procure the necessary documentation. A good-natured clerk sat smoking a pipe surrounded by piles of paperwork. I handed him the letter from the book dealer, along with my letter of recommendation and attestation as to my profession as a bookseller.

"... rendered significant service to France ... be granted every opportunity ..." he started to read under his breath.

Then, with an abrupt change of tone:

"No work permits for foreigners! As for your reference ... really! Office of the President of the Council of 1939! It does more harm than good!"

And he added in a disapproving tone:

"All these foreigners! They eat our bread and then they want to work here, too."

With that, he made a note of my name and address. That made me most uneasy. And for good reason! My actions prompted two successive visits from a policeman on a bicycle who wanted to satisfy himself that I was not working.

The residents in the hotel were most intrigued by these mysterious visits.

"Is it a departure visa he's bringing you?" one of them asked, with some jealousy.

"Is it a deportation order?" inquired another, with some pity.

At the end of January 1941, Monsieur Thérive decided to close his establishment for good.

"Only the pensions and luxury hotels owned by all those Jews can survive," he sighed.

"What?" exclaimed another in astonishment. "So, our esteemed hospitality industry is being controlled by Jews?"

"That's not what I meant. That's just what I call everybody who's getting by," replied Monsieur Thérive.

"Come on, now, Monsieur Thérive, you're not worthy of such a comment," protested the Colonel. "What an injustice to blame those worthy French citizens who are no different from you or me, and what's more, you're offending your Jewish lodgers who have sought refuge with us here in France."

"I'm not talking about *them*. They're morally upright people," replied Monsieur Thérive, magnanimously.

He knew the refugees were drowning in ever-increasing worries and concerns, prompting him to grant them a certain latitude that did not, however, leave much room for sensitivities.

He was a man of mediocre intelligence, and so his business ventures regularly failed. This lack of success had spawned an envious spirit. "The Jews have always been lucky devils," Monsieur Thérive would say. And accordingly, he allowed himself to be completely swayed by racist theories.

◇◇◇

German propaganda was well and truly rife throughout France at the time, and brought its full weight to bear on the press. Many French newspapers eloquently espoused Nazi theories. Some broadsheets were so wholeheartedly devoted to such theories that it was impossible to doubt their sincerity.

To judge by the entire pages liberally illustrated with caricatures and exposing the Jewish "problem," all of France's woes, from her lack of preparation to her downfall, were attributable exclusively to Israel.

As for the radio, which was completely controlled by the Germans, it was not content with its daily broadcast of insults against present-day Jews, so also ran a series of populist lessons on the history of the Jewish people, which demonstrated their ignominy and misdemeanors dating back to well before our times.

Books, brochures, leaflets were freely distributed, posters of caricatures were displayed in shops, in the windows of newspaper editorial offices, on walls, along fences, on every street corner.

The refugees were familiar with all this German-instigated propaganda from 1933 and recognized the dawning threat.

One day, having taken the bus from Place Wilson, I saw a young man step aboard to distribute political pamphlets. Most passengers refused them. The man distributing them shouted:

"But they're free!"

"We don't want them, even if they are free!" replied somebody.

Another added:

"Get out of here, back to Germany with you!"

And everybody laughed.

A breath of French air had just blown through.

There were others agitating, handing out propaganda in public places: in cafés, restaurants, bistros, at the port, on benches.

And then there was another incident no less poignant. In a small restaurant in Rue de France, a blond man, very well dressed, about thirty years old, was carrying on at the top of his voice, addressing the whole room.

"We've had it up to here with all these foreigners," he shouted, "all these foreigners and especially all these Jews!"

One worker, swarthy skinned, with laughing eyes and blue overalls, threw back the remark:

"Hey there! My good compatriot! You just get in from Germany? Why don't you shout us a round? You must be earning a few cents for this sales pitch."

Everybody guffawed.

The agitator hurried to settle his bill and wisely headed for the door.

"Eh! Leave then, why don't you, bastard!" the worker continued, deadpan. "You're nothing but a traitor!"

◇◇◇

The tranquility of the Mediterranean seemed immutable. Imagine, then, my astonishment when, toward the end of January, that azure-blue sea was suddenly seized by veritable transports of fury.

The gale was unleashed during the night. Violent blows against the shutters woke up all the residents, who gathered out on the terrace. The crashes they heard had been caused by trees striking the windows as they were being blown about. The garden was covered with a layer of some whitish substance: it was foam tossed up by the sea, reaching all the way up the front steps.

Waves as tall as houses unfurled onto the Promenade, crashing against the walls of the hotels and villas.

Pebbles from the beach were tossed in all directions; the flooding knocked down iron gates, destroying lawns and flower beds, as the storm tore down trees, overturning everything in its path.

The Promenade was utterly submerged for forty-eight hours; nobody risked venturing out for fear of being injured or carried off by the waves. The water reached into side streets, flooding gardens, courtyards, and cellars.

Only two days later did the sea retreat and the devastated Promenade reappear, strewn with trees and debris of every kind: branches and broken glass, benches and chairs in pieces, and everywhere piles of pebbles.

The sun came out once more, a billion glittering rays shining over land and sea.

The Mediterranean had reverted to its nonchalant tranquility, its bluish finish of watered silk . . .

It seemed to be begging forgiveness for its mood of the previous days.

The Bay of Angels was indeed laughing at the angels. It was spring and all was peaceful.

But peace among men had not yet returned . . .

◇◇◇

I had spent three months at Monsieur Thérive's pension. The announcement of its imminent closure forced me to seek alternative lodging. This time, I rented a room in a hotel in the upper part of town.

The hotel garden, with its palm trees and beautiful flower beds, was a haven of scents and shade.

It was to be my home from the beginning of February 1941 to that fateful date, August 27, 1942.

In theory, the fifth floor was accessed by a lift. There was one inconvenience, however: it never worked. Management explained that a cog in the motor was missing. They had looked everywhere, but could not find a replacement. In short, one had to struggle up the five flights on foot, but by the time I reached the final stair, I would forget my tiredness: I was repaid for my efforts by the view that opened up before me.

Getting in supplies was already proving particularly difficult at that time. As I cooked for myself, I would take up position at the earliest possible hour in the queues outside the shops and, on market days, in front of the stalls in Place Sainte-Hélène.

The two slices of meat per week, the monthly egg, the fruit and vegetables, they all required queuing, in one line and then another. Armed with my ration card and wearing a straw hat to protect me from the sun, my two baskets on my arms, I took my position in line among the housewives, the children, the young people, the elderly, the elegant socialites, women who had been swimming and simply thrown a robe over their costume to do the shopping, the women with a child on each arm, not counting those tugging at their skirts, who were sometimes children "borrowed" for the purposes of qualifying as a large family and going to the head of the queue. I remained in line, book in hand, from seven to eleven in the morning. My reward for these long periods of standing would often be fatigue and disappointment.

With the rationed foodstuffs purchased, I still had to source fruit and vegetables, which were not subject to a quota. Shop-keepers generally posted at the front of their shops, by order of the police, the quantities of goods that had arrived. In principle these were supposed to be divvied up equally according to the approximate number of customers. This policy, which in itself made sense, was not monitored. In fact, there was no way of noting on the ration cards that a customer had been served. "It would be too complicated, you'd have to keep a whole system of accounts and set up an office," declared the shopkeepers, genuinely overburdened.

Opportunists took advantage of the system by making purchases with cards borrowed here and there from various families.

Customers who went away empty-handed would protest, threatening to "loot everything." For the most part, however, they went no further. The population was too exhausted from these daily efforts to turn its mind to revolt.

On more than one occasion, I returned empty-handed, like so many others.

◊◊◊

Directly after the defeat, the disruption to the railways and all other forms of transport was at its worst. As a result, provisioning was in utter disarray.

When the armistice was announced, the authorities, statisticians, and the press affirmed that as soon as road and rail networks had returned to normal, France would be able to feed its population with the support of its colonial empire.

Once the enemy's hold had been methodically established, unforeseen difficulties emerged which stopped these plans in their tracks.

The confiscation by the occupiers of rolling stock, the division of the country into several zones, each isolated from the other (one could not even access the "forbidden zones"), the difficulties of importing from overseas, the blockade, the absence of labor—due to those deported or held prisoner—all meant that the promised self-sufficiency did not materialize.

There was another unforeseen consequence of the Occupation: German authorities would make trips into the countryside and, thanks to their very advantageous exchange rate, would pay farmers and producers unheard-of prices for their goods. These direct requisitions had very serious effects on the country's economic balance.

Goods would disappear as if by magic. I witnessed a very striking example of this phenomenon myself.

During my first stay in the Vaucluse region, good quality butter, the most enormous variety of cheeses, mounds of fruits, and vehicles laden with vegetables were everywhere to be seen.

Upon my return from Vichy, the German Economic Commission was operating out of Avignon and exerting its influence throughout the countryside. People were queuing and prices continued their relentless rise. Farmers and shopkeepers were saying: "We've no choice but to sell them everything and at any price. What's more, we're being ordered by Vichy not to refuse them any goods, and to accept their paper money! And we're being watched by their police!"

From that point on, prices already raised by the war started to spiral upward in dizzying fashion.

Hoteliers, restaurant owners, those running boardinghouses, and wealthy individuals were all contacting farmers and producers directly, offering them the German occupiers' prices.

As for the general population, people continued to wait outside shops and market stalls, but they too were turning to producers with increasing frequency. Everybody was making trips out into the countryside.

As this practice was prohibited, people would return, their mission completed, hiding whatever fruit and vegetables they had been able to find in bags, baskets, and suitcases.

In order to curb these price hikes, the authorities tried to implement clumsy measures. From time to time, they would try to impose price controls, but it was pointless, for it did not attack the evil at its roots.

Thus, massive enemy requisitioning, the lack of a labor force, transport difficulties, the blockade, derisory official taxation, and contempt for "legal" restrictions, dictated by the occupiers, all led to price rises incompatible with a decent standard of living. The combination and complexity of these issues stoked the black market.

Over time, it had become an ingenious system, run on quick-wittedness and extraordinary feats.

Manufacturers and artisans matched the price rises and for their part engaged in a system of exchange. They asked to be paid directly in foodstuffs and other products for their own manufactured goods.

And so, bartering made its appearance.

It was occurring on an ever-vaster scale and in a sense amounted to a form of revenge on the black market.

The black market and bartering each had a firm hold.

In 1943, a clandestine flyer about the provision of supplies in France fell into my hands. It revealed that 80 percent of the French population was resorting to prohibited methods and the remaining 20 percent was languishing miserably under the official rationing system.

One anecdote was doing the rounds: "Jean just died!"—"Was he ill, then?"—"Not exactly, but you know, the poor man was only living off his coupons!"

German propaganda took advantage of the situation created by the defeat, the burden of the armistice, and, most of all, by the Occupation, which was draining the country of all its reserves, to lay the blame at the feet of the Jewish refugees.

Yet, toward the end of 1942, they had disappeared from economic life, deported to concentration camps. But the black market was flourishing throughout all of France.

In the Occupied Zone, from where Jews had been deported since the invasion, and particularly in Paris, it was systematically organized. A quasi-official institution. The government never took any steps to abolish it.

◇◇◇

The hotel, La Roseraie, should have been called Noah's Ark.

It was home to survivors from the most diverse nationalities and social classes. They were a disparate lot indeed, united by their shared waiting for peace.

My neighbor from the room on the right was a Spanish woman, a Republican, who for several years had found refuge in the south of France. She would leave the hotel early in the morning and return late at night. I scarcely saw her. It struck me on our first encounter that she was unusually pale, and she grew even more so. She seemed to be suffering from homesickness. Only on the day of her death did we learn that she had slowly been starving herself. She had grown silently weaker, without complaint, never asking anything of her neighbors.

To the left lived a Jewish couple, proprietors of a spinning mill in Mannheim. They were waiting for visas for Palestine, where their daughter was already living.

If they were absent, the postman would often hand me telegrams addressed to them, and that is how we grew to know each other. Their room was full of trunks and suitcases, all buckled up and labeled. They had been keeping their luggage ready like that for two years now, they confided in me. One day, they announced they had run out of patience waiting in Nice, and were leaving for Marseille in order, they hoped, to board a departing ship sooner. I received a further two cards from Marseille. After that, I don't know what became of them.

Upon their departure, they had left me all their cooking utensils: three saucepans, five plates, several cups, and cutlery. This gift allowed me to invite some fellow lodgers to dine with me.

Thus I established some relationships that eventually grew into firm friendships.

There were also two students on my floor, who had been uprooted from their previous lives and were in sore need of some maternal attention.

One of them, Monsieur Charles Guyot, a small, sickly fellow from Lyon, was a devout young man, through and through. When Lyon was occupied, he had protested with a group of friends and had soon been forced to flee. He was living in Nice under a pseudonym. He entertained the whole hotel with his deadpan humor. The other, Daniel Léger, a Protestant, was from Paris, the son of a converted Romanian Jewish mother whose eyes he had inherited, and a French father, a doctor in the capital. Upon coming into contact with the German occupiers and their methods of persecution, Daniel Léger had suffered a nervous breakdown which Nice had not succeeded in healing. He existed in a state of constant anxiety, believing he was being pursued. The two students were friends, and would eat together in little restaurants, always trying new places in the hope of finding a better meal. On returning to the hotel, they would politely beg the female neighbors on their floor for any little extras—"to nibble on," as they would say—which were always very gladly offered. Grateful, they would then bring back whenever they could several kilos of onions perhaps, or several kilos of oranges, sometimes even their ration of wine. Their deliveries were greeted with cheers: onions and oranges were received with equal enthusiasm. They each made their own further contributions to the life of the hotel: one in the form of his witticisms, the other by his lively discussion of bigger problems, for we would all gather together to talk politics, to consider events, to plan for the future, but also to hold a sort of literary salon, where we would discuss a book, a poem, or a concert. These hours livened up an atmosphere that was all too depressing.

I shared the "chairmanship" of our floor with a Viennese woman, Madame Elsa von Radendorf, who occupied the most beautiful room on the fifth floor. A woman of letters, she had left Austria in protest at the Nazi movement. There was all the more merit in this as she was over sixty, an age where the conveniences of a comfortable home generally take precedence over ideological considerations.

Still active, she divided her time between two diametrically opposed occupations: she was writing a history of the origin and development of the art of lacework, and in addition to her advice and support, she would also offer her services as housekeeper and nurse to the young people in the hotel. At any hour, one could call by her room for a glass of wine or liqueur, an increasingly rare pleasure.

We formed a bond. At first, we were brought together by our common struggle to find enough food to eat: we would help one another out, sharing sources and methods for getting in supplies. Over time, it was friendship that united us.

The Viennese lady, who had been living in the hotel for a year, informed me that the fourth floor was occupied by Polish émigrés: an aristocratic couple, a famous actor, a man of letters who was no less well known, an art critic, and two politicians. They lived a life apart from the other residents of the hotel, full of conversation and making grand plans for the future; some of their elegant, quiet compatriots also enjoyed access to this Slavic oasis, a floor of reveries and courtesy, where the purring consonants of the Polish language were to be heard.

The third floor belonged to the emigrants. All cultured Jews—lawyers, doctors, teachers—they spent their time preparing for their forthcoming emigration. With every departure, those who remained would take heart and wait their turn with new reserves of patience.

A septuagenarian lived there who had succeeded in crossing the demarcation line in the most dramatic manner. He had set out with his son, but just as they had arrived in the Free Zone, the two men found themselves separated. When the older man learned that his son had been recaptured and sent to the Drancy concentration camp, he fell into a profound depression. His neighbors in the hotel arranged between them to take it in turns distracting him: some took him out on the Promenade, others would pay him a visit to cheer him up. But Monsieur Samuel Mendelsohn knew how to evade the well-meaning watchfulness of his circle of friends and, one night, he hanged himself from the window of his room. The door was sealed, and from then on, one hurried past on that floor. Our neighbor's tragic end resonated with us as too brutal an example of the possible fate lying in store for each of us.

The second floor, on the other hand, was enlivened by the presence of a Hindu prince. A great lover of music and dance, and a collector of records and books, he filled the floor with the sound of music and a sense of mystery.

In contrast to the rest of us, the Hindu prince was not sustained by hope and thoughts of the future alone. His was a rich and full life, so he said, devoted to beauty, nature, and harmony. Courteous and affable to boot, he offered his assistance to everybody in a disinterested, lordly manner.

The other residents on the floor were guests passing through, a special category of guest whom we used to ignore. Thus, the floor retained the imprimatur of the exotic prince.

The all-powerful management ruled over the first floor, exercising an absolute dictatorship over the residents. Right next door to the management, a single room, the most beautiful, was let to a mysterious character. Doubtless of Slavic origin, very blond with very blue eyes, and a sophisticated elegance, he not only had the looks of Narcissus, but the spirit, too. He appeared to hold court amid an entourage composed largely of White Russians, numbering more women than men. He conducted numerous businesses with the help of his subjects: he acted as a jewelry broker, and was no less expert in property, estates, vehicles, and objets d'art than in bric-a-brac. From time to time, he organized boisterous parties that would end in violent scenes.

At the start of 1942, a rare cleaning of our "up-in-the-clouds" floor seemed to herald the arrival of a significant new resident. And in fact, one fine morning, a chaplain moved into a beautiful room looking out over the Alpilles hills.

He arrived by bicycle, with a knightly bearing. A man in his sixties, he was tall with a commanding figure, courteous and jovial. He had been a chaplain at the Front from 1914 to 1918 and retained a soldierly presence despite his cassock.

His kindness contrasted sharply with his military appearance. He was charitable and, even though he trusted to Providence in every respect, he was wont to say: "God will help us if we help each other," and, indeed, he unhesitatingly offered assistance to whomsoever called on him.

I made his acquaintance in the most unusual fashion: having slipped on a step, I was spread-eagled on the landing amid the potatoes I had just brought back from the market. At the sound of the fall, my reverend neighbor rushed out and, Good Samaritan that he was, helped me back to my room, but not before gathering up the contents of my basket. I'd taken some painful bumps and bruising, but it was not the first time Monsieur the Chaplain had tended to the wounded, and he bandaged my sprained finger and then entrusted me to the care of my Viennese neighbor.

He came regularly to inquire after my well-being during the week I was confined to my room. I owed him a great debt of gratitude which I repaid in the manner of the times, namely by bringing him hot drinks throughout the colder months.

Thus passed the winter of 1941–1942.

◇◇◇

During this period in Nice, the most fearful moments came when identity papers were reviewed.

About a week before their residence permit expired, foreigners had to present themselves at the prefecture of police with their documents, one of which was a stamped application.

They would take their place in line in the Passage Gioffredo. This alley attracted an unusual draft which was often a welcome cool breeze for those having to wait there for hours on end. On rainy or windy days, however, it was truly torturous.

At last the applicants would be allowed into the building in batches of ten to fifteen, to appear before a girl sitting at a table laden with folders and piles of files. She had brown hair and was of average height. Her gestures were full of vigor: in fact, everything about her exuded a confidence which contrasted with the worried demeanor of the refugees.

She would examine the documents, bark monosyllabic queries, take rapid notes, and never respond to anxious questions. She would eye the suppliant with the grim look of one of the Fates, mistress of another's destiny. If she thought one of her subjects looked particularly downcast, humiliated, and anxious (some of them were elderly and sick, and they were all distraught, even the young ones), an ironic smile would spread across her face.

The refugees called her "the Nazi" and feared her. The haughtiness of her demeanor betrayed the fact that she was not unaware of the power she exerted over these thousands of stray souls.

She would consult her files and make authoritative decisions. She might extend residence permits by one month or three, repeatedly summon people to appear at the prefecture, ask for an additional document, a reference from a French citizen, or a medical certificate. In the meantime, she would retain the papers and one would be left, full of apprehension, with some sort of receipt in hand.

Out-of-date documents were frequently declared invalid and confiscated. It was then impossible to renew them, as communications with those countries occupied by the Germans had been cut off and consulates either abolished or left with no authority whatsoever.

Mad with worry, the person concerned would besiege the police station seeking advice, information, and support, and would end up filling in new stamped applications that were more like pleas for help. They would describe their distress, their hopeless circumstances, point out that they had means to support themselves, that they were gravely ill, infirm, and who knows what else!

Finding themselves in such difficult circumstances, some appealed to supposed "advisers," many of whom were very often crooked.

Others turned to doctors, consulted specialists, went to see surgeons.

One day, a lady from our hotel told me, radiant:

"I have nothing to worry about. I'll get my residence permit: I have to undergo an operation!"

If the refugees were unable to extricate themselves from these complications, they would find themselves in breach of the regulations and exposed to the threat of police action.

I suffered these tribulations along with everybody else. The residence permit granted to me in 1939 which was supposed to last "until the end of hostilities" was invalid following the armistice: the office of President of the Council of Ministers had ceased to exist and references issued by its departments no longer had any validity according to the new authorities.

These laborious, exhausting procedures often had their comical side.

For every application to extend a residence permit, one had to provide evidence of sufficient means to support oneself: a bank account, foreign subsidy, or cash. In the latter case, the person concerned would have to show his cash to the civil servant in person. Very often the sum available to one person or the other did not reach the prescribed minimum amount. So he would borrow from friends, acquaintances, and from neighbors in order to demonstrate access to the required amount. On leaving, he would then return the sum to the creditor who was sometimes waiting nearby. The clerks were not always taken in. One day, one of them, deadpan, said in a low voice to the refugee who was busy counting out notes:

"Is your banker waiting for you at the exit to the prefecture or at the corner café?"

It was said perfectly well meaningly, for the clerk was not taking the requirement seriously. The refugee was let off, having had a fright.

One way or another, the question of documentation ended up being sorted out and one was able to breathe again . . . until the next expiry date.

In the interim, everybody led a life burdened by preoccupations and suffering, relieved by neither work nor happiness.

The background to this existence was the waiting, a canvas upon which ever more meager hopes and ever gloomier thoughts together embroidered their nostalgic motifs.

From time to time, lighter shades would stand out against these somber colors, such as a fleeting happiness, a more gentle emotion: a letter from friends or relatives, news from Switzerland, Sweden, or America, miraculous countries where there was no war.

◇◇◇

In March 1942, the Vichy government ordered a general census.

Special posters directed Jewish members of the population to indicate their racial origin in their declarations, on pain of imprisonment.

The significance of this order was clear, since in Germany, a similar census had ushered in the era of persecutions.

Everybody realized, moreover, that it was a measure imposed on the French state by the German authorities. It was obvious what would happen next.

People were undecided as to how best to act. Some said:

"If we deliberately fail to declare our race they will obviously follow up, but there's always a chance it might go unnoticed. In that case we're safe. On the other hand, making such a declaration would definitely expose us to all forms of persecution."

Others replied:

"We're in France, a country that has welcomed and protected us. We owe her a duty of loyalty and we *must* comply with these requirements. French authorities *will never condone any atrocities against us. We have faith.*"

An atmosphere of confusion and indecision thus marked preparations for the notorious census. Then came the final day for returning questionnaires. People had to decide, had to act. Most made truthful declarations. I was one of them.

With the census complete, everybody was required to hand in their identity papers to the prefecture of police. A week later, these documents were returned, bearing the expected annotation. Then it was the turn of those affected to register their race with the Department of Supplies. Everybody was now classified, branded, "in perfect order" according to the police. The *danse macabre* could begin.

In Paris, foreign Jews started being deported from the beginning of July; in Lyon, from July 15. There was a sense of imminent danger throughout all of France, but nobody really knew how best to act.

Fugitives were arriving en masse, from everywhere, in great distress, bearing terrible news.

Refugees living in the Alpes-Maritimes region were besieging consulates: American, Spanish, Swiss, Swedish . . . They would queue up to attempt that next desperate step; but most visa offices were no longer operating.

We felt imprisoned, our path blocked.

Those who had salvaged a few possessions from a previous exodus sought to place them in safekeeping with French citizens. The most far-sighted were on the lookout for places to hide. Everybody was waiting uneasily, helpless in the face of unavoidable circumstances.

I had written to my Swiss friends saying that "my state of health had deteriorated," which, we had agreed in our letters, meant that I was in danger. My friends replied that I could count on securing an entry visa into their country.

Relying on this promise, I took myself off to the prefecture. I showed them the message I had received from Switzerland, with my 1939 reference attached to it, and requested an exit visa.

The official, a young man of about twenty, considered the two documents and told me politely, in a matter-of-fact tone:

"Madame, you have there a reference from a prewar government that proved unfit to govern. That government has been abolished. We have a new France now. The masters you served no longer exist."

I was not unfamiliar with this line of reasoning. It certainly wasn't the first time I'd heard it! This time, however, I protested, exclaiming:

"Boileau, Molière, Corneille, Racine, Voltaire . . . these are the masters I have served, monsieur, these and many other of your immortal countrymen!"

My words appeared to awaken a few schoolboy memories in the young man.

"All right," he said in a conciliatory tone after a few moments. "I shall try to lodge an application for you. Your passport, please!"

He fed a sheet of pink paper into his typewriter, spelled my name aloud, then typed it out.

"I hope you're not Jewish?" he said, with a sudden change of heart. "Show me your residence permit."

He glanced over it.

"Pointless making an application! We have strict orders not to allow foreign members of the Jewish race to leave France. This law will soon apply even to French citizens. You understand," he added, in a low voice, as if confessing, "the Germans are in charge."

He seemed to be apologizing for himself, and his attitude moved me.

I left the prefecture. I was walking with hurried steps. On the corner of Avenue Gambetta, I realized I was still holding my passport and reference.

I sat down on a bench, returned the documents to their envelope in a daze, and remained there, utterly crushed.

◇◇◇

On August 26, 1942, I went out to do my shopping as usual. Despite the early hour, it was already very warm. I was surprised to see so few people at the market.

After doing my groceries, I headed back to the hotel at a leisurely pace. I had fallen into the habit of glancing up to the fifth floor to give a friendly wave to my Viennese neighbor upon turning the corner into the little street that led back to my hotel. That morning, she wasn't there, but I did notice my fellow countryman, Monsieur Sigismond, on one of the third-floor balconies. He was waving his arms about strangely. I watched him, amused at first, thinking he must be having a bit of fun. But I soon realized, astonished, that he was gesturing at me!

I paused, trying to make out his meaning. I realized he was pointing to the lane opposite the hotel. Without trying to make any further sense of it, I headed in the direction he was pointing.

Reaching the avenue, I came upon a crowd of people. Several buses were parked there, surrounded by numerous policemen. Then some gendarmes arrived, shoving men, women, and children ahead of them or grabbing them by the arm.

"What's happening?" I asked a truck driver.

"They're picking up the Jews," replied several voices at once.

"We're hunting humans now," came the disapproving comment of one worker.

A crowd was gathering around the coaches.

Crossing the avenue, I headed instinctively for the sea. I sat down on a bench, setting my baskets at my feet.

The Mediterranean stretched out in front of me; behind me,

there was no escape. I sat there a long time, trying to gather my thoughts.

The coast road was deserted. After a while, a group of policemen on bicycles came heading toward me. I waited until they had passed and then started back toward the avenue.

The buses were still parked there and groups of two, three, four, and five people were still being led over to them. They were carrying suitcases or even just parcels. Gendarmes were shoving them into the vehicles. Two buses, filled to bursting, drove away. Two more, these ones empty, replaced them immediately.

For a moment, I was tempted to run toward the crowd, shouting, "Take me, I'm one of them!"

A feeling of intense joy overwhelmed me at the thought of such solidarity, such sacrifice. But cold logic took over.

Who would benefit from such a sacrifice? What could it change? What good would come of it?

The instinct of self-preservation had won out.

The bitterness of this truth weighs on me still, and will to the end of my days.

I do not know how long I remained there, as if paralyzed.

Somebody dashed past, bumping into me.

With a jolt, I realized the danger I was in . . .

◇◇◇

I scanned the avenue, the little laneways, the houses, shops, and villas, searching instinctively for somewhere to take cover.

My eyes fell on a shop window:

MARIUS—HAIRDRESSING SALON

I had met Madame Marius while waiting in line. One day, as methylated spirit was being distributed, she had suggested I go to her place whenever I needed any fuel. Our relationship developed around the important question of how to source supplies. For my part, I had "introduced" Madame Marius to a farm where one could source fruit and vegetables. An entente cordiale existed between us. I enjoyed stopping by for a little chat with this friendly, congenial couple in their thirties.

Madame Marius was Corsican, with eyes like embers and her black hair worn in heavy plaits. Monsieur Marius, although a southerner too, had blue eyes and brown hair. He was a light-hearted, even-tempered fellow.

The couple were as obliging as they were cheerful, and it was no surprise their salon was always full. Crowded into an impossibly small space, cramped and confined, their customers—for the most part spirited southerners too—waited their turn without grumbling, perfectly content even.

The shop was always abuzz; banter and double entendres abounded; everybody talked over everybody else, recounting the day's events, the news, and speculating about the future.

Finding myself alone, in the middle of the street and in danger, I made my way to the Mariuses' salon, as if guided by an invisible hand.

The owner was standing on the front step, he must have been watching me, for he simply said:

"Bonjour, madame, it's good you've come to us. Come in!"

And going ahead of me, he called out:

"Francine, come and see who's brought us provisions this morning!"

He shot his wife a rapid look that was like a tacit agreement.

She then greeted me, offered me a seat, went over to the *cafetière*, and poured me a cup of coffee and a glass of cognac, not forgetting to put the sugar bowl on the table, which in those times was a special mark of hospitality and generosity.

"Drink," she said to me, "the coffee is hot and the cognac will do you good."

Then she disappeared into the kitchen.

After swallowing the drinks, I brought the two baskets in to her.

"My, they're heavy!" She smiled. "That will go well with our stew."

Just then, some neighbors out in the courtyard walked past the glass door, and she gestured to me to go back into the bedroom, where I huddled away once more.

The pink mosquito net hanging over the marital bed, the old chest of drawers filled with towels, the dresser full of crockery and multicolored cups, the walls decorated with family photographs and postcards, it all conjured up a calm, welcoming atmosphere. Through the half-open door, I heard voices from the salon. There was talk of the day's events, of the big roundup; but I couldn't make out any details.

At noon, Madame Marius set the table for three. Her husband came to join us and, sitting down, he announced:

"I found out some information from an official I know. They're going to keep gathering up those poor people for several days still and then it'll be over. It's a matter of holding out for a while. And we'll hold out! Ah! The dirty bastards! They'll cop it one day."

Then, as he poured me a ladleful of soup:

"You need to conserve your strength, madame. Eat up! Times are tough, but everything comes to an end. Cheers!"

The wine helped lift Monsieur Marius's spirits. It helped him cope with all life's vexations and worries.

The meal was finished in silence. With the last mouthful of wine downed, my host concluded:

"Consider yourself at home; I mean to say, you're with decent French people here. Nothing will happen to you so long as we're in charge here. You can count on us for the future and for your revenge, so long as my name is Marius!"

Then the household returned to its work. I sat down in my corner at the back of the room. The boss's wife appeared frequently to exchange a few words with me.

At four o'clock, she brought me a bowl of café au lait. A little later, some friends, alerted by Madame Marius, came by to see me. The Viennese lady advised me not to go out under any circumstances and promised to bring me a few clothes and toiletries the following day.

Monsieur Sigismond recounted how at eight o'clock in the morning the police had burst into the hotel and arrested two Jewish couples; the others, no doubt warned away, were not there. The police had left a list of Jewish residents, ordered management to forbid them from returning to their rooms, and to bring them immediately to the local police station. My name was on that list. Just as I'd been returning from the market, three gendarmes had been standing right on the hotel doorstep, and had I not been warned by my neighbor, there was no doubt I would have fallen into their hands.

A plan of action was discussed and it was decided that I would, for the time being, remain in hiding with Monsieur and Madame Marius.

Once the salon had closed, Monsieur set about laying down a

mattress on the floor, while Madame took out some white sheets from the chest of drawers and made up the bed. Monsieur was preparing to sleep on the floor. I had to insist and even threaten to leave in order to ensure the two of them remained in their own bed.

At last, Monsieur Marius said to his wife:

"If that's what she wants, so be it, Francine."

And so the white sheets were moved from the bed to the mattress where I was to sleep.

I listened for a long time that night to noises outside.

Hurried steps, muffled exclamations, whistles, shouts . . . and once again the murmur of the sea.

I tossed and turned, unable to fall asleep.

"Sleep, dear lady, you need your rest," came Madame's soft words, catching me awake and anxious.

I buried my face in the pillow to hide my tears. I was weeping in despair, but at the same time, out of gratitude toward these infinitely kind souls who had taken me in and saved me.

The realization that I was safe there, with them, calmed me.

Exhausted, I finally dozed off.

◇◇◇

The owners awoke rested and ready for work, which, for both of them, was their whole life.

Monsieur Marius was an idealist who dreamed of peace and universal brotherhood. He loved to talk for hours about humanitarian issues. Both husband and wife were sensitive to the misery and sorrows of others, were always in agreement, and were constantly ready to offer help to all who were suffering.

They spared no effort in their care and consideration of me.

In order to distract me, Monsieur Marius enlisted me in a game of cards in the evenings, which I regularly lost. I genuinely admired his skill, which pleased him enormously. Madame Marius, for her part, was proud of her husband.

These evenings were really very pleasant and they helped me to bear, even to forget, momentarily, my tragic and dangerous circumstances.

Elsa von Radendorf returned often, bringing with her terrible news.

The police were rounding up people at night. Sweeps to flush people out were organized in gardens, parks, the squares, on the beaches, in the surrounding woods. On the assumption that most of the fugitives, after having gone into hiding outdoors, would slowly return to their homes, the police burst into scores of rooms, tearing residents from their beds and taking them away. Thus, it was impossible to return to my hotel room to retrieve anything I might need. Elsa von Radendorf, however, brought me a few items purchased in haste—a toothbrush, soap, handkerchiefs, stockings—and lent me her dressing gown. She also agreed to post a letter in which, under a pseudonym, I informed my Swiss friends that I was "critically ill."

Every day for the next week, roundups were rife throughout the Alpes-Maritimes. Many people were arrested; you saw them walking, handcuffed, between policemen. Police, gendarmes, and members of the Mobile Guard were locking them up in police stations, barracks, and in the covered market in Place Masséna. All of these places were hastily transformed into temporary prisons.

At the start of October, everybody had to renew their ration cards. Police were present at the offices to collar those who, having escaped the roundups, were now coming for those indispensable coupons.

But there were few who turned up. Instead, it proved an opportunity to arrest those French citizens who came, out of pity, to collect the coupons of those in hiding.

◇◇◇

Shortly afterward, a new measure was instituted: Jewish children were to be removed from their parents. They were thrown into trucks, their papers torn up on the spot. The authorities branded them with an identification number.

Tragic scenes accompanied the implementation of this measure. Mothers cut their wrists, others threw themselves under the buses just as they pulled away with their tragic cargo. In one hotel on the Côte d'Azur, a woman who had escaped the roundups threw herself from the window with her young child. When they picked her up, her legs were broken. The child was dead, crushed in the fall.

Police and gendarmes were on the hunt, displaying inexhaustible levels of skill and energy. They implemented the Vichy regulations strictly and inexorably. These subservient men harbored a violent anger accumulated in the wake of the defeat, and it was as if they wanted to take it out on those weaker, less fortunate than themselves. There was nothing heroic about these agents of authority, not their job nor their approach.

Some deep sadistic urge must lie hidden in every man, waiting to be exposed when the opportunity arises. It was enough to have given those boys, quite gentle enough in themselves, the abominable power to hunt and track down defenseless human beings, for them to carry out the task with a peculiar and savage bitterness resembling joy.

Were they just carrying out orders or acting out of a sense of shame? One heard them claiming that the procedures were useful and necessary, since it was one of the conditions of collaboration with the Germans, and France's salvation depended on that collaboration.

It did not take long before final decisions were made regarding the Jewish refugees who had been arrested. For a week, friends were able to see them and bring them some basic necessities, a little comfort. But one day, without warning, they were taken away to the French concentration camps, and from there transported, according to their category, to camps in Poland, Czechoslovakia, and Germany.

◇◇◇

I had some qualms about remaining hidden with the Mariuses, but each time I spoke of changing my hiding place, my hosts protested; they considered it their duty, they said, to counter the injustices in which their fellow countrymen, whether blindly or compelled by the authorities of the day, were complicit.

The couple's bedroom was adjacent to the hairdressing salon. Some clients were in the habit of going through to exchange a few words with Madame Marius or to wish her good day. Thus, some of them had seen me and soon there were rumors that the Mariuses were concealing somebody in their home.

It had been agreed that when Monsieur Marius called for his wife in a very loud voice, I was to hide myself at the back of a cupboard.

This happened one day around midday, and from my hiding

place to which I had swiftly retreated, I heard Monsieur Marius say:

"Come in, Sergeant, it's just the bedroom and kitchen we have. The inspection won't take long."

Then, turning to his wife:

"Why don't you offer the sergeant a glass of cognac. Let him tell us if he likes it."

The sergeant drank his glass of cognac and, excusing himself, said:

"You know, it's driving us mad. All day long we're passed information and denunciations. It's a dirty job we have now! Running after people who haven't committed any crime, it's enough to make you sick! But you can't say what you think. We'd be locked up on the spot. We have to feed our families. No hard feelings, boss!"

After excusing himself from his host, the sergeant disappeared.

"You see?" said Monsieur Marius to me once I had emerged from my cupboard. "There are still some decent sorts among those damned police pigs."

That was how I happened to discover (a fact that had been carefully hidden from me) that the homes of French citizens suspected of harboring hunted Jews were being subjected to searches. Police were turning up day and night, forcing their way in if necessary, arresting any refugees they found there and taking their hosts away with them.

Notices informed people of the risk of penalties and imprisonment facing charitable French citizens.

I had asked friends to inquire about a refuge for me outside Nice. Realizing the danger in which I was placing the Mariuses by remaining there, I no longer had any peace. I was very pleased to learn one morning that a French lady from a good family had said she was prepared to let me shelter in a cottage in the grounds of a château in the mountains, about twelve miles from Villefranche.

My hosts protested. However, faced with my firm resolve, which was supported by my Viennese friend, Monsieur Marius agreed to my leaving, but only on the condition he meet with my new hostess beforehand. It was decided that the chatelaine, the lady of the manor, would come to collect me herself from the Mariuses' the following Sunday.

Generously sheltered in my warm, comfortable refuge, I waited, somewhat anxiously, for the second stage of my extraordinary journey, almost like some adventure from days of yore.

During the last two days I spent with them, my friends outdid themselves spoiling me. Madame Marius ventured out to some farmers and brought back eggs, impossible to find in Nice, and even some lemons. Digging into her cache of white flour, my hostess baked a beautiful tart in my honor.

Madame Elsa von Radendorf, too, arrived triumphantly; she had managed to access my room at the hotel, and had come away with a dress, some shoes, a coat, and a few changes of undergarments.

My neighbor from the hotel, the student from Lyon, Monsieur Charles Guyot, suggested I seek advice from an officer of the peace whom we knew personally. Originally from Alsace, this policeman loathed the occupiers. He used to visit Monsieur Guyot; I had met him several times, and he had assured me I could rely on his support in the event of complications. Not knowing quite how to undertake my move to a new hiding place with an expired residence permit, one with the dangerous branding of my racial classification, I decided to follow the advice of my young neighbor. I wrote a brief note to the police officer. I reminded him of who I was, setting out my difficulties.

A friend of Monsieur Marius was tasked with bearing the note. I awaited the results with feverish impatience. As for Monsieur Marius, every second saw him at the doorstep to check the messenger had not returned. It was afternoon when he returned, and in what a temper. He recounted that having duly handed the letter to its addressee, he had been hauled over the coals most unpleasantly right from the outset. The officer had started by asking to see his identity papers, following which he had said to him:

"What! You, an ex-serviceman from 1914, you're compromising yourself by getting involved in these unlawful matters which contravene our government's policy?"

And he had concluded with this advice:

"Whatever you do, don't try it again!"

At first, I didn't want to believe my ears, but the description the messenger gave of the man who had interrogated him matched in every respect the description of our supposedly good friend and, ultimately, I considered myself fortunate to have been let off so lightly for having taken such an inopportune step.

VII

Somewhere in the mountains

The following Sunday arrived, and with it our chatelaine, who was supposed to bring me to her home, near Ville-franche. She was in her forties, with a masculine look about her and a cold expression. She told us she had a daughter and a son. The property, heavily mortgaged, belonged to friends living in Paris; they had allowed her the use of it for twenty-five years, provided she bear the costs of maintenance and taxes.

She shared her political opinions with us, her anger toward the Germans, and demonstrated her satisfaction at being able to come to the aid of a "victim of persecution." She confirmed that, far from acting out of self-interest, she was nonetheless hoping to get some benefit from this lodging arrangement, for times were difficult. We set out the situation for her and fixed a price for rent which was equivalent to that of a luxury hotel on the Promenade des Anglais. As for foodstuffs, my friends would have to procure them for me. Monsieur Marius was privy to negotiations, and while he did not appear overjoyed with the chatelaine, he nonetheless agreed to these terms. He even threw in the promise of two packets of cigarettes per week, after the chatelaine had demonstrated during the course of the conversation that she was an enthusiastic smoker. It was a very attractive offer. Tobacco was strictly rationed and it was only available to men.

Thus, we were agreed on every point.

I set about donning my disguise: a broad skirt, woolen slippers, an apron, and, covering my head, a peasant's shawl that fell to my shoulders. On my arm I would be carrying a basket containing a few provisions. My toiletries were handed over to the chatelaine to avoid suspicion.

We set off at around six o'clock in the evening. After a very emotional farewell from Monsieur and Madame Marius, I followed my guide.

We boarded a tram. It took us to Place Masséna. There we were supposed to wait three quarters of an hour before taking the bus that serviced the area surrounding Villefranche. The chatelaine used this time to pay a visit to somebody nearby, leaving me alone at the bus stop.

There were lots of policemen and gendarmes about, on foot and on their bicycles. Suddenly, right before me, a young man flashed past at full speed, two policemen hot on his heels. They caught him and put him in handcuffs. I saw him walking off between the officers, back hunched, head down, his gait unsteady. He disappeared around a street corner . . .

When the chatelaine returned, I felt genuinely surprised to

still be there: in my mind, I had been taken along with the young Jewish man who had just met his fate.

The bus climbed unhurriedly up into the hills. While my hostess, who was very chatty, filled me in on life at the château and told me about the neighborhood, I took in the magnificent scenery of the Alpilles, which I had not previously seen from this vantage point: fields, woods, little villages that seemed to cling to the verdant hillsides.

Now the chatelaine was talking bitterly of her neighbors, complaining about their selfishness.

"The area is teeming with workers," she was saying. "I'm surrounded by hostility, for most of them are Communists. As for the local police? They have the same leanings."

As I listened to her, a certain uneasiness crept over me: my hostess seemed at odds with the entire universe.

We got off at Place de la Mairie, directly opposite the gendarmerie. Its walls were plastered with faded notices about the census and more recent posters forbidding the harboring of Jews. In order to get to the château, one had to walk uphill for about two and a half miles. My hostess suggested I make the trip slowly on my own and that I wait for her at the crossroad, so we would avoid being seen together.

The footpath was cut from the rock itself and there were many steps to struggle up. Little houses and cottages were built higgledy-piggledy, lining the path the entire way. A few villas stood out here and there; further away, small farmhouses, surrounded by olive trees and palms.

I progressed slowly, stopping to admire the view.

At last I arrived at the specified crossroad, in the middle of which was a fountain. I told the chatelaine, who soon joined me, that as I made my way up, I had been seen by some people who had greeted me with a friendly "Good evening" from their front doors. She reassured me: people often came to visit in this part of the world and indeed never a Sunday passed when she herself did not receive visitors from Nice.

The château was surrounded by beautiful lawns carved out among the trees. The building was in clear need of restoration, but it was of very distinguished design.

I was introduced to a young blond woman of about twenty, welcoming and mild-mannered, and a boy who might have been sixteen.

I was offered, by way of lodging, a room decorated with two beautiful Gobelin tapestries. Four big balconies opened up to a view of the Alps. But as soon as night fell, the château was enveloped by such heavy shadows that I hurried, anxiously, to close the shutters and turn on the lamps.

The following day, dressed in one of the chatelaine's aprons, clogs, and a straw hat, I went into the orchard to pick vegetables. I gathered large stones from a field that the chatelaine was planning on sowing. Then I carried them in a basket to a designated spot.

In the meantime, my hostess and her daughter turned the soil over. When the hottest part of the day had passed, we watered it, carrying the water from a pond. Using special gloves, the young man stripped caterpillars from the trees and threw the insects, in their hundreds, into a brazier. He called me over to show me the caterpillars squirming in the flames.

Several days went by, peaceful and calm. I felt as though I was at the end of the world and that I would be safe forever. But one Saturday, returning from the village where he had gone to fetch bread, the young man recounted that he had run into one of the three local gendarmes who had asked him, in a low voice, to come by the gendarmerie. He had stopped by there half an hour later. There, he was told of a rumor in the village: a foreign woman was said to be living at the château. The woman had not yet registered with the police. The officer had finished by saying:

"My colleague and I will come by to carry out an inspection on Monday morning. The person in question will have to have left by then."

The chatelaine lost her head on hearing her son's account and thought I should leave immediately. I asked if I might at least have twenty-four hours, enough time to notify my friends in Nice so they could find me another place to shelter. Would I not risk being arrested and deported by heading back down toward the town?

I asked the chatelaine's son to take two letters, one to the Mariuses and the other to my hotel neighbor.

He set off and returned toward evening, telling me that Monsieur Marius would do what was necessary and would come up to the château immediately.

After dinner, the chatelaine came to see me in my bedroom. She had had a conversation with her son, she told me, "the only man of the house." She had not realized the danger to which she had exposed herself by offering me lodging. Knowing the attitude of the police toward her, she could expect serious repercussions! The gendarme had just issued her with a warning, I reassured her. But all she saw was a trap on the part of the police.

It was decided I would have to go into the forest next to the château, where she promised to organize a safe place to shelter. We headed off into the woods, carrying blankets and a cushion.

When we arrived at a little gully, the chatelaine pulled out some ferns which she then arranged so as to conceal me.

I was left all alone.

I had brought a book with me and I tried to read. But I couldn't focus my thoughts. I was surrounded by a muffled silence, interrupted by the last of the birdsong and the humming of insects. I listened, and watched night descend over the forest; the last rays of sunshine painted the tops of the trees gold; the sound of voices floated over from distant houses; little by little, the birdsong faded away.

Night came and enveloped me like a shroud. The silence was broken by soft noises, scarcely perceptible: leaves, twigs, pinecones dropping from the trees. A bird brushed past a branch with its wing, an insect climbed the trunk of a tree and fell back to the ground. The wind seemed to whisper in the foliage. All these noises took on sinister implications. The barking of a dog on some unknown farm sounded almost like the voice of a friend.

Suddenly, I was struck by the cold and I huddled under my coat and blankets. I tried to sleep, but to no avail. I tried to conjure up a comforting thought. But what? My beloved mother was far, far away; I had had no news of her or any of my family for two years; the whole world was stained by the blood of war. Everywhere, loss and despair. I thought of the Mariuses, of my Swiss friends, of my sister, already out of danger. I was soothed by their memory.

Thus I remained for hours on end, looking into the darkness. That night seemed as if it would never end.

At last, reddish arabesques of light appeared in the sky. I felt the gentle warmth, still weak, of the sun's first rays on my face.

My hair was damp with dew and I ached all over from having slept on the ground.

Dawn was breaking. The dew was sparkling now on every branch, on every blade of grass. The pale light of the dawn gave way to a dazzling brightness. One, ten, one hundred, a thousand birdcalls grew in volume in an early morning chorus.

Day had arrived. My distress dissipated. I took in my surroundings admiringly.

Suddenly, I was gripped by fear. Somebody was walking along the path. Heavy steps were approaching. Should I flee? In what direction?

Soon, an old woman appeared among the trees. I lay down flat against the ground, but she had already seen me.

"Good morning," she called out, cheerfully, "so people are still out camping this late in the season? It's going to be a beautiful day."

On she went.

Shortly afterward, the chatelaine's daughter came to find me. She appeared quite overjoyed to see me there and told me she had not been able to sleep peacefully thinking about me all alone. I told her immediately that a local woman had caught me by surprise. She left to warn her mother and the two of them then returned.

"Nothing but trouble!" cried the chatelaine, annoyed. "Had I foreseen all these problems, I would never have accepted this task. No, indeed!"

In the middle of the forest stood a former gamekeeper's hut, now used for storing gardening tools and broken furniture, including a folding bed.

It was here the chatelaine took me.

I was frozen to the bone. The young woman brought me a

pitcher of warm water so I might wash, as well as some coffee and bread. She quickly dusted off the folding bed and went to fetch a mattress which she covered with blankets.

I was still shivering with cold. Feeling sorry for me, she helped me into bed, fully clothed. She locked the cabin up so if people should come looking they would not find it open, then she left, promising to return.

For a long time, I tried to warm myself up. At last I fell asleep, troubled by nightmares.

At noon, I heard a noise in the lock, the door opened, and, like a guardian angel, Monsieur Marius appeared before me. He had just made the journey by bicycle and had been soaked by a shower. He told me that after having taken delivery of my provisions for the entire week, including two packets of cigarettes, the chatelaine had announced I would have to leave immediately.

"In the name of G . . . !" he swore, squashing two fat spiders scurrying across the floor with his heel. "Some château you've landed in, isn't it!"

Taking a seat on an old box, he told me he had done the rounds of his reliable friends, but at every turn there was a hitch. Sometimes the neighbors were "pro-collaboration," sometimes the son in the family was working for the police. He suggested I return to their place in the meantime.

Then he went to negotiate with my hostess and it was decided I would stay the night in the hut, which would be swept and tidied, and then I would leave, once and for all, the following afternoon. He settled the rent.

All of the week's provisions—meat, wine, ten kilos of potatoes, as well as the cigarettes—were to remain with the family by way of compensation.

Monsieur Marius commented to me:

"They're annoyed to see you leave because you were a source of supplies, and at the same time, they're fearful about keeping you. I have the impression," he added, laughing, "they wouldn't be at all unhappy if you were to continue to pay them rent and bring them supplies . . . even after you've left. That would suit them nicely!"

He suggested I join him in taking a little walk in the forest to stretch my legs. And again he did his best to lift my spirits during our short walk.

When he left, I even found myself hoping that everything might work itself out. Back in my cabin, I started to read. In the evening, Noiraud, the cat of the house, came to visit me, and the young woman left it shut in with me to keep me company.

The next day, I got up with newfound energy. I needed it, for the walk down into the village where I would take the bus back into Nice from outside the gendarmerie constituted an obvious danger.

The chatelaine and the young man appeared at the cabin in the morning. The son asked if they could rely on my loyalty; he feared I would reveal the last place I had stayed if I was arrested. They emphasized again the danger involved in the gendarme's visit. So, I asked for something with which to write and penned a letter to the chatelaine, setting out that, not having informed her of my race, I had taken advantage of her hospitality in seeking accommodation at the château, and that I was leaving her house without her knowledge to avoid causing her any trouble.

I was then allowed to spend the remainder of the afternoon at the château.

At around five o'clock, I dressed in my disguise once again.

Carrying a milk can and a basket full of tomatoes, I took to the main road.

At the crossroad, near the fountain, I spotted Mademoiselle Yvonne, the chatelaine's daughter, who appeared to be waiting for me.

"Allow me to accompany you for a moment, madame."

And falling in step, she continued:

"I didn't come with my mother to bid you farewell as I didn't want to witness all the odious suggestions my brother was still proposing to foist upon you. Please, madame, do excuse my mother! She is very much influenced by her son! And he is young, he can still change, can't he, once life has returned to normal? Dear God! What must you think of us? I am so ashamed! I'm French, I abhor such cowardice! I was raised in a convent. We're Christians! Although you wouldn't think so!"

Stopping, emotional and out of breath, she said:

"Madame, allow me to embrace you."

She wrapped both arms around me.

"I would have liked to accompany you all the way to Nice, to be sure you were all right, but they would notice my absence; then I would never hear the end of it."

"Best of luck, Mademoiselle Yvonne, I will never forget the kindness you've shown me," I said to her, embracing her in turn.

I quickened my pace and turned back a moment later to wave goodbye one last time to the young woman, who had stopped to follow me with her gaze.

I walked quickly, eyes and ears alert, nerves taut, but accompanied by an inner happiness: I was reliving the young Frenchwoman's farewell.

◇◇◇

Before me, a magnificent view: here, bare, arid rocks; over there, verdant mountains, vast fields of flowers, olive trees, palms, lemon and orange trees; the whole floral spread of the south of France. My God, how beautiful it was!

The fanciful curves of the roads cutting through the fields, meadows, and countryside looked like white ribbons designed to accentuate the beauty of the scenery.

The air rising off the fields filled my lungs, the sun warmed me through once more with its gentle, autumnal rays.

> To whom God will His favors show
> Shall far into the world be sent . . .

I was walking along to the rhythm of my song as I neared the village. I slowed, then, to cast a glance around: the road led to Nice, and police patrols looking for fugitives were common.

Another fifteen hundred feet. I stopped. A dot appeared in the distance. It was approaching at great speed. There was no possible doubt. It was a motorcycle. I picked up my pace again so as not to attract attention by the hesitation in my stride and headed toward the motorcycle, its gleaming steel clearly visible now.

I heard my heart beating and tried to swallow the knot I felt in my throat.

The vehicle grew rapidly larger. It had taken no time to reach me. The noise of the accelerator . . . Already it was long gone . . .

◇◇◇

Who is this woman in disguise, walking with a spring in her step and singing a childhood tune under her breath?

I am that peasant woman in her clogs, humming along in time to her steps as she walks down the white road through the wondrous countryside.

VIII

Return to Nice

It was Sunday. The local roads were busy with people out and about. On reaching the village, instead of waiting for the tram at the main stop, I continued to the next one. In doing so, I skirted around the gendarmerie and found myself out in the fields. But here was an unexpected mishap! The little tram was packed and didn't stop. I had to get on the next one. An anxious half an hour on the main road. But I was not arrested.

At the gates to Nice stood a tollhouse where officers were inspecting parcels and baskets; I endured this formality somewhat fearfully, even though I did not, in fact, have any rationed supplies in my bag.

I got off at the stop at Place Masséna where Monsieur Marius was supposed to collect me at around seven o'clock. In my haste, I found myself at the meeting point three quarters of an hour early. Out of habit, I started counting the policemen passing through the square on foot, on bicycles, and on motorcycles. I had counted twenty-eight when, at last, I spotted Monsieur Marius on his bike. He gestured to me to follow him and took a side street where I then met up with him. Pushing his bicycle as he walked alongside me, he suggested I take the tram to his place and come in through the courtyard, after I'd made certain there was nobody near the entrance. In any event, I was unrecognizable in my disguise so I could go directly there. Even he admitted he had not recognized me at first.

The moment I stepped over the threshold of the Mariuses' home, I was overcome by a feeling of absolute safety. Fears and dangers were forgotten and the persistent tension with which I had been living disappeared as if by magic.

I started to tell Madame Marius about my odyssey and I felt my mood lifting on hearing her laughter at my description of the chatelaine and her son.

Then we sat down to eat. Monsieur Marius told us about his latest discovery: a young sewing machinist, who was working for the big ready-to-wear clothing stores, was subletting a room in her little flat. Her room had just become free, she could take me in. But there was one drawback: this young woman had male friends, some permanent, others more temporary. It was problematic, but all things considered, he had decided to broach it with me because this solution did have major advantages. The woman concerned had indicated her delight at the opportunity. The fact that her home had, one might say, a "somewhat public" character, allowed one to suppose that the police would not be carrying out any searches there for the time being. Mademoiselle Marion—that was her name— was supposed to stop by that very evening to get a response.

❖❖❖

Marion was a woman of about thirty, tall, thin, elegant. Her dark hair and eyes, her wide, sensual mouth, her slightly vulgar beauty lent her a singular attractiveness.

The room price she set was the same as that demanded by the chatelaine and, as you would expect, we agreed.

I wanted to leave with Marion, but Monsieur and Madame Marius decided it would be better, for safety reasons, to wait until the following day. Madame Marius and I left at five o'clock in the morning, before the police had appeared.

Marion's apartment was near the Gare du Sud railway station, in a new building with modern amenities. She was very house-proud. Two windows looked onto the street and one onto a small courtyard. I was given the back bedroom. In the room was a divan covered by a tapestry with a foliage motif, a small table, and two stools; at the windows, brightly patterned drapes. Half curtains hung stretched across the windowpanes to deflect the curiosity of neighbors. If I wanted to air the room, I was supposed to approach the window on my knees and, in that position, reach out my arm to pull on the cord. A Turkish-style rug, bought from a North African *sidi*, completed the décor.

Once I had moved in, I realized I had co-tenants: three female cats and a tomcat. Marion adored cats, but she did not want to let them into the "salon," which doubled as a bedroom. Thus, the feline family found itself relegated to the subtenant's room. Marion assured me no other tenant had ever had the slightest objection to these cohabitation arrangements.

My very particular circumstances meant I had no choice but to follow the tradition set by my predecessors.

I was fond enough of cats, but in smaller numbers.

Thus, I fell asleep with my companions, one across my shoulder, the other next to my head, and the last two across my feet. The slightest movement of an arm or leg on my part was interpreted as an invitation to play hide-and-seek, and sometimes, in the middle of the night, my bed served as an arena for a festival of leaping and bounding that quickly banished any tranquility.

The price I had to pay for this cohabitation was a bed and clothes covered in hair and, alas, fleas. My personal hygiene regimen was inadequate to rid myself of these calamities. I had to ask Madame Marius to buy me an insecticide powder for use on the cats and a special comb to attack the evil at its roots, a process which allowed me to give my four companions a thorough clean. Marion appeared very touched by my somewhat forced devotion, and from that point on, moreover, the cats' attachment to me was settled! They never left me alone again!

The doorbell rang often at Marion's place. Her visitors had various ways of ringing, from one to six rings, with different rhythms. The sound of the doorbell would make me start, particularly if I was alone. It goes without saying that I refrained from opening the door.

Fortunately, my bedroom was separated from the rest of the apartment by a corridor and a heavy curtain. I was able to read and write as I pleased without being too troubled by the comings and goings.

Every day, one of the Mariuses would bring me something to eat. At an agreed time, I would go into the kitchen, which, by the way, was immaculately clean, in order to eat my meal. We would both sit down at the table, surrounded by purring cats trying to scavenge some tasty morsel from our plates.

Marion liked money, but as she told it, it was because she knew all about "life and the treachery of men." She told me about her past, her trials and tribulations. She had a good heart, but was utterly lacking in moral fiber. Despite her outward display of friendship, she would soon demonstrate a susceptibility to nefarious influences.

One afternoon I was writing a letter to Madame von Radendorf, who had stopped visiting me following my most recent move in order not to attract attention. Marion came through to my room and, as she approached, she whispered:

"There's a fellow from the police at the door. He wants to speak specifically to you. You can imagine the fright I had when I saw him! I denied you were here, but he told me he knew what was going on and just wanted to give you a warning."

Without waiting for my response, Marion had already gone again, and was letting in a man who looked somewhere between twenty-five and twenty-eight years old.

"Don't be scared," he said to me with a broad smile as he came over and sat down on a stool. "I've just been demobilized," he started; "I was in the navy and they've stuck me in the secret police for the time being. Now my job is to search out refugees in hiding. I've been on your trail for a good while now. I've finally tracked you down! But you're a woman, I feel sorry for you. I'm prepared to hold my tongue . . . You probably realize what keeping silent like that means? I could be punished, imprisoned! You do understand what I'm saying, don't you?"

"You'd like some form of compensation?" I asked him.

He spread his arms:

"I'm taking a huge risk, madame."

"How much?" I said.

"Seven thousand," he replied, laconically.

I was struck by the sum. It was exactly the amount I had just been offered three days earlier for my typewriter. (It had been confiscated at the hotel on police orders, along with the rest of my personal effects. One of the hotel residents had offered, through friends, to buy it from me, unaware that I no longer had it.) Marion knew all about the matter. I was astounded by the coincidence, and the thought of her possible complicity flashed through my mind.

There was a moment's silence. I had to make a considerable effort to stand up. Going to the door, I opened it and called out:

"Mademoiselle Marion!"

She was standing right outside.

"Marion," I said, "my hiding place has now been revealed. Sooner or later it had to happen. Pass me my coat and shawl. I'm going with this gentleman to the police station."

"But come now, madame," she cried, "since Monsieur is being so obliging, you're not about to turn yourself in, and us along with you."

"Monsieur is not risking a thing," I reassured her, "he's only doing his job. He'll get the usual reward. Every denunciation gets a bonus."

"And what about me? I've hidden you and cared for you!" she cried, desperate.

Just as I was heading for the door, she grabbed me by the sleeve. I freed myself in disgust. Then, turning to the fake policeman, she begged him:

"Louis, come on, aren't you going to stop her?"

And she burst into sobs.

The young man pushed her away, made for the door himself, and ran down the stairs, four at a time.

I had to assume he would denounce me.

I told Marion to take the tram and go to the Mariuses to ask what I should do. Quite beside herself, she left.

The girl's complicity was soon evident, as no police officer appeared. Or perhaps the illustrious detective was sparing her!

It was well and truly dark when Marion returned. She brought word from Monsieur Marius, telling me to come that very evening, after the blackout, and to have Marion accompany me.

The two of us waited for ten o'clock to arrive without saying a word. The cats circled us, exercising all their charm in an effusive display of affection. It was as if they wanted to reestablish the ties formed by weeks of shared living, ties that had just been so miserably torn asunder by their mistress's weakness.

◇◇◇

When, at around eleven o'clock that night, we arrived on foot cloaked in darkness, the Mariuses were waiting for us impatiently. Monsieur Marius told Marion to stay with his wife until he returned.

He left, taking me with him, and without saying a word led me toward a nearby alley where he spoke in a low voice to a silhouette standing in the shadows.

"Good evening, madame, we're late. We'll explain why later. It's good of you to have waited for us."

Then, turning to me:

"Go with this woman, we'll follow around midnight."

I walked in silence behind the woman, who was taking care to walk quietly in her old shoes. We turned two corners and went into a building. My new hostess was keen not to turn on the light and we had to walk up the stairs by the light of our torches. On the third floor, she opened a door and allowed me to go in first. The light flashed on and . . . I found myself standing before one of my dear acquaintances, Madame Lucienne!

How great was my surprise. We embraced. She took me through to the beautiful room she had readied for me.

I must have caught a chill, for I started to shiver and my teeth started to chatter. Madame Lucienne helped me undress, gave me a woolen nightdress, and quickly prepared a hot water bottle and a herbal tea.

At about midnight, somebody scratched softly at the door. It was the Mariuses. At the sight of these two, and their evident loyalty, I dissolved into tears. My disappointments, my bitterness, all of it vanished, erased by an immense feeling of gratitude. They too seemed moved, for however great the joy of being saved, even greater must be the joy of those noble souls who come to the aid of a human being in distress.

We chatted, made plans, and that night I slept calmly.

Madame Lucienne had been a nurse for twenty-five years in a hospital in Marseille, where she had devoted herself body and soul. After she retired, she had taken herself to Nice, the place of her dreams, where, with her small savings, she had been able to create an intimate, cozy retreat. She had adorned her home with all she had been deprived of during her quarter century of hard labor. Cheerful fabrics, plentiful cushions, and amusing ornaments enlivened the décor; brightly colored hummingbirds, canaries, budgerigars, a talkative green parrot, a blackbird, and even an injured sparrow, taken in out of pity, filled two cages or fluttered around the room.

There were flowers everywhere, at the windows and filling

numerous vases on the tables inside. The apartment was full of scents, song, and gaiety.

Tall, sturdy, very dark-haired and with kindly brown eyes, Madame Lucienne wore bright dresses, long, dangly earrings, large, showy brooches, and, on seven out of her ten fingers, rings set with colorful stones.

Widowed in her first marriage, she had since been twice divorced. Men, she said, disappointed her.

I had met her some time ago in my little restaurant. She, all in color, me, all in black; we had both felt an unusual connection.

The numerous years she had spent dealing with bureaucracy had molded her spirit into that of a civil servant. She believed only in authority and official regulations. She respected the police, whom she believed to be dedicated solely to the suppression of crime and the tracking down of criminals. Her daily paper, in which she placed a blind faith, was a source of spiritual nourishment. Her radio and newspapers provided her with a ready supply of political opinion and worldviews. She did not care to think too hard, she'd say, and gladly accepted ready-made judgments. Genuinely convinced of Marshal Pétain's ability to act freely and of his complete understanding with the victors, she had a naïve trust in the political direction of the day.

At the time of the persecutions, she had initially been upset, for she was fundamentally a good person. But the Jewish history lessons she listened to on the radio, the "age-old crimes" of these people, had led her to admit that the measures in question, while troublesome, were probably necessary. We had fallen out over this point of view.

How great my astonishment, then, to find myself suddenly face-to-face with her. Knowing I was in danger, she had been going to the Mariuses regularly to find out the latest on my situation. That very day, they had told her somebody had tried to blackmail me. She had then exclaimed:

"I trust our government, since the Marshal is part of it; but I feel sorry for this woman who has always seemed honest and decent. I can't believe she's a criminal. Bring her to my place."

And that is how I found myself at Madame Lucienne's.

Appreciating how she must have struggled with her own sense of discipline and her beliefs, I was all the more touched by the sacrifice she was making on my behalf.

A high fever kept me bedridden for a week. I really was very fortunate to find myself living just at that moment with Madame Lucienne, a first-class nurse and carer.

A pleasant friendship developed between us. She would care for me. We read. I would teach her a card game, but she would forget the rules from one day to the next. I would scold her for being absentminded. She would make a visible effort, but without any effect, I might add.

She preferred to make me listen to records. Each one prompted a sentimental memory which she would recount in melancholic fashion.

A relative—a retired office worker—was living with her and she took me under her wing too. These two women, from a conservative family, loyal to the administration, showered me with their attentions, each jealous, it sometimes seemed, of my friendship with the other. But at the same time, they were conscious of "contravening the laws of the day" and they felt the scruples of their model civil servants' consciences. It was a case of "two storms within two minds."

However, their well-meaning French hearts appeared to have

won out. Each time Radio Paris set out the grounds for racial measures, Madame Lucienne was visibly anxious about the legitimacy of her conduct but, glancing furtively at me, she would turn the dial, saying:

"Too bad about that provision of the collaboration!"

And we would exchange a smile of "entente cordiale."

In order not to attract attention by carrying luggage, I had left Marion's place without taking a thing. Two days later, Madame Marius went to fetch my clothes. Marion handed her a suitcase with a few bits and pieces in it. As for the dresses, they had disappeared!

After my departure, Marion explained, she had taken my belongings to the cellar, fearing a search. That morning, knowing that Madame Marius would come by, she went to retrieve the suitcase but found it had been forced open and the two dresses were no longer there!

The Mariuses had been almost beside themselves before coming to tell me about this latest pillage. But it was not the time to make a fuss. One had to put on a brave face. As was his wont, Monsieur Marius promised:

"They'll pay for this, all of them! After the war, as Marius is my name!"

Madame Lucienne and Madame von Radendorf each offered me something to wear.

These touching displays of kindness and loyalty were an invaluable support.

◇◇◇

I was paralyzed in a state of agonizing anxiety about my mother and the rest of my family, not having had any news. Cooped up, with no possibility of going out, unable to exercise, and without any fresh air, I suffered such insomnia that my nervous strain was becoming unbearable.

All I had by way of entertainment was Radio Paris and my hostess's French newspaper! I was constantly bombarded by both of them with stories of Allied defeats and of the collaboration reaching its apotheosis. Not a ray of light nor hope to be had there.

The threat of danger remained. There were daily arrests. On one occasion, the police seized some unfortunate soul in the middle of the street who had ventured out, driven by an overwhelming need for space or exercise, or to carry out some important and urgent task.

Some risked their freedom just to immerse themselves for a moment in the atmosphere of the town once again.

Several times there were arrests in front of the Swiss and American Consulates, where refugees would go to see if a visa or notice had arrived for them. For none of them had any fixed address where they might be reached.

Every time a new hiding place was discovered, the newspapers reported it and took the opportunity to warn the population about the danger they courted in continuing to assist refugees.

I was constantly thinking about how to move closer to the border, from where I wanted to try to flee across to Switzerland. I feverishly carried out the preparations for an escape, with the help of friends in Switzerland and Nice.

I would have remained in hiding with Madame Lucienne until I was able to leave, were it not for two incidents that compromised my safety there.

The apartment looked onto gardens and a field. As I never

went near the windows, nobody was able to see me. One day I was sitting at the table in the middle of the room, reading, when I had a feeling of being watched. Perched on a tree outside, the concierge's husband was busy picking figs. Seeing I had noticed him, he greeted me. Madame Lucienne frequently entertained visitors and my presence may not have surprised him. Nonetheless, this incident caused us grave concern.

A few days later, a clumsy mistake almost gave me away.

Cut off as I was from the outside world, friends would come to pass on urgent messages, deliver letters, a public notice, a word of advice, news of political developments from foreign radio broadcasts, or simply to chat about trifling matters from the outside world.

They wanted to show solidarity and provide encouragement. In order not to attract attention, there could never be too many visitors. Each person had to get in touch with the Mariuses ahead of time and take advantage of an appropriate moment.

And so it happened, one Sunday, after blackout, I was waiting for a visit from an old neighbor. He had just returned from a reconnaissance trip carried out on behalf of his friends. He had traveled all over the Isère and Savoie regions and was coming to pass on useful information for the implementation of my plan.

When he arrived at the door to the building, he noticed a woman in the shadows. He approached her and asked if she were waiting to direct him to the Polish lady. The woman, who was in fact the all-powerful concierge, replied that there were "no foreigners in the building, just decent French citizens."

Conscious of the blunder he had just committed, my visitor excused himself and left, intending to return a little later.

Sure enough, the concierge went up from floor to floor to

announce to the tenants that somebody was looking for a foreign woman who, it appeared, was hiding in the building. Naturally, she also came to us.

I'll never forget poor Madame Lucienne's expression, both anxious and full of regret. She came rushing into my room and kept repeating, "This is bad . . . this is bad . . . this is bad!" as she paced agitatedly up and down the room, wringing her hands.

She told me the whole building was on high alert. I had to leave, then, before word reached the police station.

As always, the Mariuses were informed and I found myself— for the third time—returned to my appointed benefactors.

They received me with their customary kindness and un-assuming courage. Even though my successive retreats to their home were always the result of some disaster, I still felt elated every time I crossed their threshold. Their inexhaustible concern made me feel completely safe.

◇◇◇

The railroads, the highways, every form of traffic was controlled by the German authorities and the French police who were carrying out their orders. At the entrance and exit to railway stations, in front of ticket counters, on platforms, at the main bus stations, at the toll barriers on the outskirts of town, travelers were interrogated by gendarmes and their papers were inspected. On the trains, German police in civilian clothes would pounce on people, sometimes more than once on the same journey. On the roads, every vehicle was pulled over, from expensive cars to carts pulled by donkeys. All foreigners were forbidden to leave their home unless armed with a safe-conduct pass. That docu-ment was not issued to foreigners of Jewish race, and yet they had to risk escape, whatever the cost; it was the only path to salvation! It was an intractable dilemma.

Every refugee was thinking of fleeing to Switzerland, Spain, or England. They resorted to methods as ingenious as they were dangerous. Plans multiplied and were perfected over time.

The most courageous simply set off, traveling at night, taking cover during the day in bushes, in the woods, or with charitable hosts. Numerous French families were offering shelter. A comprehensive organization sprang up with cells in every town, its own covert communications, messengers, information networks, and even luggage transportation services! Sometimes, when it was impossible for them to continue on their way, fugitives would stay for days, weeks, even months with their French hosts. And they not only hid them, but found ways and means to feed them. This was a tour de force in and of itself, for these unfortunate souls no longer had ration cards.

One could write volumes about the courage, the generosity, the fearlessness of those families who offered assistance to fugitives in every *département* and even in Occupied France, putting their lives at risk. It was not unusual for generous-spirited French citizens unhesitatingly to lend their identity papers to refugees,* allowing them to travel without a safe-conduct pass.†

In November 1942, a new decision stipulated that every person traveling had to carry ration papers as well as an identity card. This was serious, for if a French person could survive for a

---

* French identity papers used to clash with the foreign accent of those holding them. In the event of an inspection, the subterfuge was blatant. Searches quickly revealed the fugitives' real documents, retained in anticipation of what lay ahead.

† In June 1943, this freedom was restricted when the requirement to carry a safe-conduct pass was extended to French nationals.

time without identity documents, it was not possible to go long without a ration card.

A new industry was thus born and soon grew widespread: the manufacture of these documents for use by fugitives; an industry supplementing the one that already existed for identity cards.

People would choose the names of French citizens living a long way away, in the forbidden zones, in the colonies, or abroad, wherever it would be impossible to carry out an inspection. False identity papers were also useful for those who had to abandon the idea of escape. During the Occupation, many foreigners trapped in France by the war hid behind such names, whether they were Jewish or simply nationals of countries at war with Germany—English, Belgian, Dutch, Norwegian, Polish, or Russian. They had no need to procure a fake ration card, for the genuine civil status they had acquired entitled them to an official document.

These documents, issued by skilled draftsmen and engravers, sometimes achieved perfection in their imitation, and commanded fantastic prices, too! The prices varied according to circumstance: a fresh upsurge or a slackening off in persecutions. Some people liquidated their assets and sold off parts of their wardrobe in order to acquire these indispensable documents.

Clandestine French organizations soon issued the documents for no charge, proffered advice and useful information, and supplied the necessary money and clothes to those arriving without anything.

This work drew upon covert financial subsidies, and people were aware that these came from leading French religious and secular figures.

In December 1942, the Vichy government doubled the

number of police, increased security measures, and tightened its surveillance. Barbed wire was reinforced everywhere. Police dogs were used for the first time.

In the end, nobody dared risk traveling alone on the roads. So people engaged guides who knew which trails and secret tracks to take, the streams that were easy to cross, and the most sheltered mountain paths.

These guides had numerous "tips" and relied on assistance from locals, and even in some instances the complicity of gendarmes and customs officers. They were the masters of a new form of trade, human trafficking. The profession of "people smuggling" had just been born.

Whenever an expedition failed, the fugitives were taken to the nearest police lockup where, after serving their time for unlawfully attempting to cross the border, they were sorted according to age and nationality and sent to French concentration camps or to fortress detention. From there, a new sorting process would result in their final deportation.

◊◊◊

The French camps included Noé, for the elderly, the sick, and the infirm, as well as Récébédou, near Toulouse, Masseube (in Gers), Rivesaltes (in Pyrénées-Orientales), the Rabès internment center (in Corrèze), and Gurs (in Basses-Pyrénées) for Jews from Germany, Holland, the Grand Duchy of Baden, and the Palatinate.

From 1941, this last camp took all the foreign Jewish refugees, with no distinction as to nationality.

Of all the camps, it was the most terrible, a veritable hell. In the winter of 1940–1941, between fifteen and twenty-five people per day died of exhaustion, disease, cold, and epidemics. The camp at Drancy (in Le Bourget) ultimately gathered Jewish foreigners who had been living in France for a long time, as well as more recent refugees intended for deportation.

Frequently prisoners in French camps were liberated by virtue of the most varied forms of intervention. But nobody ever returned from Drancy, which was under the direct control of the German authorities.

◇◇◇

News of accidents, thefts, blackmail, arrests, deportations, and failed escape attempts spread rapidly throughout the region.

Consequently, the number of escapes fell very quickly. Exhausted by the hardships they were enduring and weakened by their long confinement and the resulting inertia, the refugees had been sapped of their energy. Escape felt like a considerable undertaking with all-too-unpredictable results. Resigned, they ended up passively awaiting their fate, abandoning their plans and, at the same time, all hope.

Only an intrepid few, particularly among the young, preferred to brave the perils. They set off, carrying deadly poisons, weapons, or, absent those, a dose of sleeping pills sufficient to kill them in the event of failure.

If somebody had an entry visa for another country, there would never be any hesitation about setting off.

I was waiting for just such a visa for Switzerland and, in order not to compromise this possible path to salvation, I was forced to remain in hiding in Nice for some time yet.

◇◇◇

There was a beautiful new house in Cimiez where two ladies lived on the fifth floor. They bore an astonishing resemblance to each other: tall and thin, they fed off their mutual likes and dislikes. Both mother and daughter had started taking on knitting work to make ends meet following a reversal of fortune. In these times of war, the cost of their rent unfortunately exceeded their means, so they were looking for a subtenant. For my part, I was once again looking for a safe haven. Thus, we were a good match.

In fact, they were not at all willing to give up a room, as each of them planned to keep her own.

At last it was agreed I would sleep on the living-room sofa and would rise early to guard against the possibility of an unexpected visit.

I am keen to acknowledge that these two women were hardworking, frugal, excellent housekeepers; patriotic to the point of chauvinism, they suffered from two unbearable failings: the first, the flip side to their excessive patriotism: xenophobia; the second: envy.

They revealed themselves to be constantly envious of everything: of a letter or money order sent indirectly through a friendly contact in Switzerland, of a visit, or a show of sympathy, kindness, or readiness to help. They were envious of my provisions, envious even of any hope, any joy, rare as that was in this dark period of my life. They wished only to see me in my normal state, that is, hunted, demoralized, and desperate.

They never missed an opportunity bitterly to inflict their sour moods on me. Without a room of my own, I had no place to be alone. Such opportunities were, as a result, frequent . . . constant, even.

◇◇◇

The arrival of the Italians in the Alpes-Maritimes *département* appeared to be the result of some ad hoc decision. Hour after hour, convoys of artillery, infantry, mountain troops with hundreds of mules, followed by trucks and ambulance vehicles, made their way down the Promenade. The Italian headquarters were set up in a luxury hotel in the center of town.

An unexpected piece of news soon spread: thanks to the intervention of the Holy See, the occupiers had just decreed that persecutions be immediately suspended.

The synagogue of Nice, which had been defaced with vulgar inscriptions, its windows broken, was cleaned, restored, and returned to being a place of worship.

Jewish refugees were asked to register themselves at police stations and to go to the prefecture to renew their identity cards and residence permits; all landlords were ordered to return whatever property they'd been holding. The Jewish community was informed of the Italian occupiers' policy of protection of the Jews. Thus, those refugees who had survived the roundups were to be seen waiting outside the prefecture. They were only a small group.

Issuing as they do from a long line of persecuted ancestors, having been tormented and dispossessed for generations, Jewish people have an undeniable instinct for danger. Despite the liberal attitude of the Italian authorities, they were wary of what the future held. Everybody took advantage of this lull to prepare their escape to the Creuse, the Isère, and especially the Savoie regions in order to be closer to the Swiss border.

◇◇◇

I took advantage of the respite offered to everybody by the Italian Occupation to put my affairs in order. Like everybody else, I went to renew my residence permit as well as my identity card and ration card. At both the police station and the prefecture, I was cautious not to give my true address: I gave that of the hotel where I had previously stayed.

Free to move about once again, I hastily prepared for my departure. There was no longer anything keeping me with the two knitting ladies from Cimiez. So I went to live in a villa at the bottom of an abandoned garden, with a septuagenarian Parisian woman whom I had known for two years by then.

Anticipating future persecutions, which I considered inevitable, I cloaked my comings and goings with a thousand precautions, trying not to be seen, not to attract any attention.

First of all, I had to scrape together all my available assets into cash. The hotel had returned my three suitcases. So, I set about selling my belongings including my typewriter and a ring. I sold everything I could, item by item, for nothing could be allowed to impede the escape I was planning.

I filled a small suitcase with three dresses, a few undergarments, some essential items dear to my heart, including some photographs. This bag was to join me in Switzerland.

Yet again, I bade farewell to my three vagabond suitcases, whose extraordinary adventures I have already had occasion to recount.

On December 15, 1942, I took myself off to the Swiss Consulate to inquire whether my visa had arrived. After consulting some dispatches, the secretary pulled one out that related to me.

I felt overwhelmed by a complicated emotion of joy mixed with anxiety. I was acutely aware that this journey toward the border would lead either to salvation or perdition.

The Consulate's secretary stamped my passport in an amicable fashion, warning me that "of course, the border was closed for the time being." He knew as well as I did that this fact had absolutely no bearing on me: I was unable to leave France in a lawful manner in any case.

Now all that remained was for me to get hold of the identity card and ration card of a Frenchwoman. My landlady was aware of all the difficulties I was facing: she declared herself ready to help, there and then. She told me she had twice mislaid her own papers, but the police had only issued her with an official warning, no doubt due to her advanced age. Her two cards had been renewed in return for payment of the customary fine.

My hostess was going to "lose her papers for a good cause this time," as she said. Like so many French people, she vehemently opposed the government's actions and the horrors taking place in her country. I was the beneficiary of one generous gesture after another!

Before all else, I had to undertake the complicated task of transferring over the details of my own description onto the documents of my benefactress. How much effort, how much patience and attentive, skillful care it took to remove the descriptions of age, height, eye color, face and nose shape, and substitute my own.

By a stroke of misfortune, my benefactress had a wart on her chin! This particular feature stood out on her face and, much more seriously, featured in her description. How often a funny—if not to say comical—passage is written into life's drama. My friends and I spent a week or so anxiously pondering this decorative detail.

Ought I to fit myself out with a fake wart? Unfortunately,

there were none among us with the skill to produce such a thing and, in the end, we were left with no option but to erase the bothersome description, at the risk of leaving behind evidence of having scraped something off the document. Feeling extremely nervous, but displaying infinite skill, we somehow managed to remove that particular description, taking a thousand precautions.

Then came the no-less-delicate task of detaching the photo, which was solidly glued onto the card, and replacing it with my own. This task, too, required some considerable time as well as a good deal of patience.

Of course, I was taking on her surname, first name, and place of birth. Henceforth, for reasons of necessity, I would be known as Blanche Héraudeau, born in Paris, Rue de Clichy. The stamp of the prefecture was supposed to lend the final touch of authenticity to the document. It was drawn on with a paintbrush! Of course, recognized specialists had imitations of the real stamps, and some were able to access the official stamp itself, but all of that came at prices too prohibitive for me.

In the end, the documents were very presentable, provided one did not examine them too closely . . .

◇◇◇

I had all my French documents in order and the Swiss visa on my real identity card, which was sewn into my coat. I learned my new name and its spelling by heart and practiced imitating the signature of my benefactress. With my nerves stretched to breaking point, but my courage bolstered by my Swiss visa, I considered myself among the privileged and was ready for the journey.

The Mariuses, for whom I had become a sort of fragile vase that they had grown used to moving from place to place with touching care, agreed that they could not allow me to depart on my own. Never! They then found themselves arguing over who should accompany me. Madame Marius, with her angelic candor, seemed hardly the best qualified for possible encounters with the police. On the other hand, any prolonged absence on the part of Monsieur Marius would have set tongues wagging in the neighborhood.

Once again, Providence came to my aid. Fate seemed determined to lead me to salvation.

One of the Mariuses' regulars mentioned in conversation that he was going to spend the Christmas holiday period on his property in the Isère. Monsieur Marius immediately devised a plan to put me in touch with him. He knew his client to have decent French values and he spoke frankly of my situation.

Monsieur Jean Letellier, an architect by profession, an ex-serviceman, and a Republican, moreover, said he was prepared to assume responsibility for my safety and came to see me. The details of the journey were considered and decisions made. I would go, under the aegis of my new protector, to Grenoble, where he would stay with me for as long as necessary.

It was just prior to Christmas and the trains were packed. We had to fight to get seats, but in the end we were successful. It was agreed that my companion would take care of the luggage, hand our tickets to the inspector, and, as far as possible, respond to any questions asked.

The train was not heated and Monsieur Letellier spread a large travel blanket over our knees, laughingly saying:

"We'd be able to pass for a couple going on holidays. Let's pretend to be in love."

This beginning seemed to bode well for the journey ahead.

My traveling companion was the perfect man for the circumstances: of good French stock, he looked like a Gaul, without the mustache, it goes without saying. He was wearing a lambskin jacket and matching cap, and could have been a lord of the manor returning to his estate.

The journey passed without incident until we reached Marseille. Everybody was buried in their books. From time to time, I would break off my reading in order to remind myself of my first and second names.

Tickets were inspected without incident. But then, at Marseille, three clean-shaven individuals with grim expressions appeared and demanded our papers for proof of identification. Without rushing, I held mine out to them when it came my turn. Feigning indifference, I smiled at a charming young woman sitting opposite me who was fussing as she hunted for her documents, which she finally found . . . in her handbag.

Monsieur Letellier told me later that my smile, at that moment, had seemed both appealing and daft, and that he had struggled not to burst out laughing. I thanked him from the bottom of my heart for calming my anxiety with a joke and for displaying an apparent lack of concern, despite his own fears.

Twenty minutes out of Grenoble, a second inspection. This time there was an incident. A lady whom we subsequently discovered to be Belgian, and whose papers were in order, was asked by the Gestapo agents to produce her baptism certificate.

"I'm forty-two years old, I've needed my baptism certificate four or five times during my life, but it has never occurred to me to take it with me when I travel."

"You're a foreigner and your papers make no reference to your religion," replied one of the officers.

To which the lady replied:

"But I have a safe-conduct pass! Have you noticed anybody handing out safe-conduct passes to Jews in these times we're living in?"

Just then, another traveler interjected:

"I have known Madame for several years. She's my neighbor. I'm a factory manager at C—— and here's my business card. Her husband owns a factory in Charleroi."

The policemen did not persist. They disappeared to pursue elsewhere their hunt for the game they were stalking.

It is not hard to imagine my own emotions during this exchange.

IX

Grenoble

We arrived in Grenoble in the middle of the night. As it was just before Christmas, the hotels were very busy. We were only able to find lodgings in a large hotel, where the Italian Commission also happened to be located.

Monsieur Letellier inspired such confidence in the porter that he was able to fill out our registration papers without having to produce our documents.

We stayed there for several days. There wasn't the slightest hitch. I didn't bat an eyelid when I came across representatives of the occupying authorities on the stairs, in the foyer, or in the restaurant.

I had been told about a secret organization in this town which was operating in a fairly secure manner throughout the *départements* of Isère and Savoie. Armed with the password,

I was to make my way there and find an experienced guide.

One evening, at six o'clock, I found myself at the organization's headquarters, having had the greatest difficulty in the world locating it in an old, half-demolished school.

An elderly man took down my real first and second names, as well as the address of my friends in Switzerland and in France, "to be able to warn them in the event of any misfortune," and recommended I try, if possible, to get hold of some hiking shoes, some woolen stockings, and a flashlight. Then he gave me an address in an area on the outskirts of town. I was to make my way there that very evening at eight o'clock to receive all the necessary information.

At the agreed hour, then, I presented myself at a villa, where I was greeted by a gentleman in his forties who had a determined, energetic demeanor. He examined my papers, both real and fake, as well as my Swiss visa. I handed over the sum of money intended for the smuggler. He gave me the final instructions.

◇◇◇

I was supposed to be at the entrance to the railway station at eight o'clock in the morning. I was to follow a young man in a worker's smock, who would be carrying a loaf of bread so I could pick him out. We were at the rendezvous at the agreed time and, indeed, leaning nonchalantly next to the entrance, we saw a worker with a large, fancy-looking loaf of bread under his arm. I say "we" because Monsieur Letellier was still accompanying me on this final leg of the journey.

The worker boarded a train headed for Annemasse. We took a seat in the same carriage, but in a neighboring compartment.

At each stop, we monitored the platform to see if our cicerone had disembarked, which he did after several stops.

We got off the train. The worker walked out of the station and we followed. After walking for a quarter of an hour, we saw our man move off to the right side of the road. Two girls and a boy, laden with a complete set of mountaineering equipment, followed suit. And so we continued, each keeping a certain distance from the other. At last our guide stopped in front of an inn, lit a cigarette, and entered. The three young people went past the house, walked around it, and disappeared through a door giving onto the courtyard.

We continued awhile down the road, pretending to hesitate between the restaurant situated a little further on and the inn. Then we too went in.

The landlady led us discreetly toward a little room where the table was set. The young man disguised as the worker set down his bread, approached us, and introduced himself as working for the fugitives' assistance association. He offered us a seat at the table while we waited for the smuggler and suggested we have something to eat ahead of the long journey on foot awaiting us.

We sat down. A few minutes later, a woman accompanied by two children came into the room. Whereas the boy, who was about ten, sat himself down at our table, the mother led the young girl, who would have been about fourteen, by the hand, as one would a very small child, and gently sat her down next to her brother. The young girl had typically Jewish features, but expressed in their purest form: her skin was the complexion of alabaster, her large, dark eyes were deep and velvety, her hair was bluish-black, framing her fine features with curls. But the child's expression was strangely distant, almost absent.

They were served promptly, for their smuggler was due to appear at any moment. The boy ate with the healthy appetite and insouciance of his age. The girl sat, immobile, and her mother started to spoon-feed her. She told the landlady, who was moved to pity, that the young girl had been in that state since the night when she had been woken by a great racket and witnessed her father's arrest.

"I've been to see a doctor in Grenoble. He assured me she will return to normal. In Switzerland, there are specialists who will certainly heal my sweet Rachel," she concluded with a sigh.

Monsieur Letellier said in a distressed voice:

"Merciful God in Heaven, and these things are happening in France!"

Just then, a man came into the room—a local fellow from the surrounding countryside by the look of him. The mother stood up, followed by the boy, gathered up a meager parcel, took her disturbed child by the hand, and waved us goodbye.

The tragic group disappeared after the man, heading for salvation . . . or deportation.

We remained silent, each one of us deep in our own thoughts.

Our smuggler was late. At two o'clock, our young guide began to grow nervous. He went to consult the owner of the inn and returned, scarcely reassured.

Finally, the landlady, having headed out in search of information, returned to announce that Monsieur Charles was nowhere to be found in the village.

"As long as nothing has happened to him. He's a man of his word and always on time down to the minute," she sighed. "I suppose there's always Julot, he's here. Do you want to talk to him?"

"Julot? Julot?" answered the young guide. "What a nuisance. I was instructed to make contact with Charles. I don't know what to do. Telephone him? That's impossible. It would be even more dangerous to take this lot back to Grenoble. There's no going back. Send me Julot. I suppose I must know him, but he's no Charles. He's brilliant, that one. I'm in a right fix now!"

He was very distressed. As you can well imagine, we were growing uneasy.

A quarter of an hour later, a man came into the room. His appearance alone made me take a violent dislike to him. Disheveled, with a dirty face and hands, he was brash and vulgar in his expressions.

"If you don't want me, you can guide yourselves. It's always Charles . . . Charles this and Charles that . . . Well, you can have Charles, then! I'm sick of this miserable job! I'd much prefer to go and have some fun in the village."

Our guide steered him through to a neighboring room. They negotiated for a good while. When they returned, Julot spoke to us as follows:

"We have to get going right away. It's winter, the sun disappears quickly. Listen up: I'll go ahead, sometimes on foot, sometimes by bike. You'll follow, but keep your distance, of course. If I stop, catch up. If I sit down on the side of the road, or crouch down, that means danger. And you'll head into the woods, but no rushing. Understood? If the cops pull you up and ask for your papers, show them, of course, no hesitation, politely. If it's all fine, you keep going and pick me up a few hundred meters further on, behind a tree. But if those bastards don't like your papers and take you away, I don't know you, never seen you! You don't tell them you had a guide or where you were going. You don't know me. Getting me arrested won't do anybody any good and it'll only hurt your friends who keep arriving every day and who we're saving. Smugglers, they're worth something these days! Agreed, ladies and gentlemen?"

"Agreed," we replied.

I was not the slightest bit convinced of the chances of our expedition's success under such leadership. It's a curious thing that, despite being acutely aware of the serious error we were about to make by placing ourselves into the care of this man, I allowed myself to do it! I heard Monsieur Letellier telling Julot that he was to take my identity papers, which he would have to give back to Monsieur Letellier later, because he would be waiting at the inn to hear how the expedition had gone.

I have often asked myself *why* I agreed to follow this smuggler who filled me with such loathing and mistrust. I think it was because of the desire, stronger than anything else, to be done with it, not to think anymore, not to look for anything anymore, to submit. I was the drowning person giving up the fight, abandoning herself to the elements.

The young people loaded themselves up with their rucksacks, their duffel bags, and blankets. Mechanically, I gathered up my bundle.

◇◇◇

"Let's go, let's go," Julot hurried us along. I thanked my companion from Nice warmly for all he had done for me. I took my leave from him, feeling very far away, almost as if I were only half-awake.

"Let's go," Julot was insisting.

As I walked past him, I was struck by his breath, which smelt strongly of alcohol. He must have had a great deal to drink.

Again, this observation left me indifferent. It was too late, it was all too late. Blind destiny would decide the rest.

We set off on our path. The sun was pale, the countryside utterly white, the snow firm under our feet. We followed Julot for three miles, the young ones and I, keeping a distance of three hundred feet. Once we reached a collection of houses, he stopped and waited for us.

"How about a little lubrication for the next five kilometers?" he said in an encouraging tone.

I handed him a banknote and he went into the little inn. We carried on, slowing our pace. Julot soon caught up.

We set off again, more briskly. After an hour had passed, my companions had left me a considerable way behind. I caught up with them again at a crossroad. Julot was waiting for me before issuing new instructions. I asked them not to get too far ahead so I would not lose sight of them. One of the young women replied:

"Everybody should walk at their own pace. We're not out for a stroll."

The other one chided her:

"Come on, Suzy, we have to look after Madame. She's not as young as us."

For a good while, everybody walked less hurriedly. But half an hour later, my young companions were far ahead, out of sight. I continued along the path, then I caught sight of Julot at a bend up ahead, leaning on his bike, surrounded by the younger ones. He announced:

"We're about to get to a tunnel. We go through it. Then there's a viaduct. We go along that and then the path starts again."

Turning to me, he added:

"When we leave the viaduct, before entering the village, I'll stop. That's when you'll hand me your papers which I'm supposed to give back to the gentleman at the inn ... As for the village, you'll go straight through it. You're tourists, and tourists are common around here. Once you've passed through the village, you get to a railway track. You stop near the level crossing and then you're there! I'll show you where you go off to Switzerland. Has everybody understood?"

"Understood," came four voices in reply.

Fifteen hundred feet further on, we entered the tunnel. Soon we were in complete darkness. Happily, we had taken the organization's advice and equipped ourselves with flashlights.

It's hard to imagine what it was like walking through the darkness!

The stones on the railway track gave way under our feet. Julot went ahead of us, carrying his bicycle on his shoulder, striving to maintain his balance. The young people were only a few feet ahead of me now. We stumbled continuously. One girl lost the heel of her shoe and stopped to rip the other one off. I was finding it more and more difficult to make progress. I fell on more than one occasion.

A feeble light grew larger in the distance. We were approaching the exit. Once out, we stopped to get our breath and looked around us.

Below us, in a valley, was a town.

"Geneva," whispered Julot to us.

And he set off across the viaduct, pushing his bicycle.

We followed him. Here and there some sleepers were missing. The viaduct was clearly not intended for pedestrian use. A dry riverbed, covered in stones and rocks, stretched out below. Overcome with dizziness, I tried hard not to look down into the abyss again. I started counting sleepers to focus my attention.

Through sheer force of will, I managed to focus only on them.

Once again our feet hit solid ground. As if suddenly unshackled, the young people set off down the path with renewed energy. I was quite simply exhausted, completely spent.

The sky was growing dark. The day was drawing to an end.

Julot stopped.

"Your papers," he said.

I gave them to him. He put them in a tree trunk which he seemed to use regularly as a hiding spot, for out of it he pulled a pack of cigarettes and an envelope.

We set off once more.

My feet were so swollen I was no longer able to keep up with my companions. I sat down on the edge of the path to take off my shoes, which were painfully tight. However, seeing everybody rapidly pulling further and further away, I stood up and started walking again in stockinged feet across ground that was hard and white with frost. Fortunately, I had found and purchased particularly thick woolen stockings in Grenoble, but I think I would even have walked barefoot had it been necessary. Without shoes, I was able to speed up.

A light mist descended over the landscape.

Countless lights glimmered in Geneva, which appeared to be drawing closer and closer. But around me it was dark. I walked by the soft light of my flashlight as if in a dream, my mind wandering, heavy with fatigue, my spirit absent. I continued along the path following Julot's instructions: I reached the village, circled past the fountain, and found myself at the level crossing.

Just silence. Nobody!

My companions had disappeared. They seemed to have vanished ...

I hesitated, no longer knowing which direction to take. I was shivering. I used the break to put my shoes back on. Surely I was at the spot where Julot was supposed to point out which way to go once we had crossed over the tracks. But the mist was so thick I could no longer make anything out.

For a moment, I considered retracing my steps, retrieving my papers, and heading back to the inn; but at the same time, I knew I would never make it.

I felt an indifference verging on utter abjection, such was my physical exhaustion. Suddenly, I dozed off.

I awoke by some subconscious effort. The short respite had restored a little of my energy. Accustomed now to the darkness, I vaguely made out a road turning off to the left. A few steps ahead of me, the silhouettes of trees rose up along the edge of a ravine. I was unable to make anything out further ahead. I entertained the thought of exploring the ravine to see where it led.

No sooner had this plan formed in my mind than I found the place working a strange attraction over me, a mysterious fascination. I was feeling my way forward . . . when, all of a sudden, a bright light struck me in the face, dazzling me. Closing my eyes instinctively, I heard a voice call out to me in a bantering tone:

"What are you up to here, in the middle of the night?"

It was a customs officer.

"Are you looking for your friends who went on ahead of you?" the man continued. "Come on, they're waiting for you."

He took me by the arm.

It took us no more than about fifty steps to reach the customs office. I saw the barrier gate in the lamplight. On the other side, a few feet away . . . Switzerland.

X

At the border

We came into a large, crowded room where there were two customs officers, several gendarmes, and a German soldier. The customs officer who had arrested me said jovially:

"Here's another one to add to that last lot! She's part of the group belonging to the smuggler who disappeared."

He was rubbing his hands vigorously in front of the stove and seemed very pleased with his "mission accomplished."

I was taken into a neighboring room, where two gendarmes were sitting at a table laden with paperwork. In pride of place sat a typewriter with a blank sheet of paper ready to go. I saw my companions sitting on the benches along the wall, utterly defeated.

What happened over the next several hours feels like a bad dream now. In it, forming a wretched group along the benches, are two girls in tears, a dazed-looking little boy, and a woman, worn out from exhaustion and cold, all of them in ragged shoes, their clothes and hair in disarray, haggard expressions on their faces. Two strapping soldiers in French uniforms are interrogating them endlessly: "Last name? First name? Origin? Race? Religion? Nationality? Prior convictions? Papers? Reasons for travel?"

The men ask the questions severely, full of self-importance, as if genuinely expecting an answer. Yet they know what to expect, having heard it a thousand times before over the last months!

"Escaping the threat of incarceration in Germany," answers a girl whose curly hair frames a tearful, pretty little face.

"Escaping the threat of being sent to a concentration camp," explains the other little one, who is not beautiful, but has an intelligent look about her.

"Escaping to be reunited with Mama, who is already in Switzerland," says the little boy, simply.

"Escaping the threat of deportation," I say when my turn comes.

Diligently, busily, the two gendarmes take our statements. There's the click-clacking of typewriters. Additional questions, interminable replies.

It lasted two long hours, then the men started to flag. Opening a door, one of them shouted:

"Search them and be done with it. It's already past our dinnertime. I've had it up to here with all their dramas!"

A woman of about thirty, with a cheerful face, came into the room. The gendarmes left, taking the boy.

After ordering us to undress, the woman first set about inspecting our clothes. She meticulously ran her hands over the seams and thicker parts of our dresses and coats, going through the pockets; then she ran her hands through our hair and made us lift our arms.

"Come on, cough up! You've got to be carrying jewels, gold, precious stones, currency . . ."

At the same time, she whispered indulgently in my ear:

"Mother Marie here isn't wicked. She'll give it all back to you when you return."

"Return from where?" I thought.

"They're going to bring you some hot soup. You'll be needing it. Come on, get a move on! Declare your valuables, your jewels. Come on, cough up!"

She ended up removing a locket from one person, and a ring, earrings, and a wristwatch worth twenty-five francs from somebody else. She took my two rings and gave the lot to two gendarmes who came into the room. The next shift was about to start.

"All there is left to do is continue with the list of jewelry we've found and the contents of the parcels. The arrest documentation has already been drawn up: they were trying to make a run for it into Switzerland without authorization. There's even one here with a Swiss visa. There's not much luggage. There won't be much to do."

The new gendarmes started going through our "luggage," placing the contents on a table in full view.

In addition to the humble jewelry taken from us, our bags and wallets were also emptied. Various random items were lined up: banknotes, coins, some underwear, dresses, combs, brushes missing half the bristles, a book, a cracked mirror, some hand-kerchiefs, and photos of friends and relatives, photos brought along after considerable hesitation, for fear of compromising somebody.

From time to time, one of the gendarmes would stop to ask the meaning of a document or letter, or the purpose of a particular item. One of them was dictating, the other typing: "One brooch . . ." "One brooch." "Sixty francs and thirty centimes." "Sixty francs and thirty centimes." "A pair of scissors." "A pair of scissors." "Ten fifty-centime stamps." "Ten fifty-centime stamps." "Earrings, a silver comb." "Earrings, a silver comb." "Three hundred francs, two rings, underwear, a dress . . ." "Three hundred francs, two rings, underwear, a dress . . ."

It was a monotonous and pitiful litany. Sitting on the bench, my head leaning against the wall, I dozed off.

"Hey! You there!" Suddenly I was being called.

I woke with a start.

"What's this supposed to be?"

He was referring to an old coin Madame Lucienne had given to me when we said goodbye to each other, telling me it was a lucky charm. I offered up the requisite explanation.

"A coin, a sort of lucky charm," he then dictated.

"A coin, a sort of lucky charm," the other one repeated.

And the typewriter continued its click-clacking: "tip . . . tap . . . tip . . ."

The second team of gendarmes started to lose patience then too, having been so zealous to begin with. One of the men called the neighboring police barracks to ask for instructions as to what they should do with us. They chatted on for some time and we picked up, among other things: "For as long as this has been going on, it's always the same story. Well then, send Marcel over with Sergeant Camus. Off they go!"

They lit up some cigarettes and stopped work. The room was full of smoke. Their "civic duty" done, their attitude toward us changed.

Meanwhile, the dinner promised by "Mother Marie" was brought in in a basket: soup, vegetables, and bread.

An officer appeared, followed by two members of the Mobile Guard, Marcel, and Sergeant Camus. This latter might have been about fifty. He had an aristocratic, intelligent face. I observed him while the other two officers, who had completed the statement and drawn up the list of our property, explained our circumstances.

The officer listened to this report with visible discomfort.

"Good, good," he said. "Have they had anything to eat? Air the room then, it reeks of tobacco. It's too late to transfer them! These women can hardly stand upright any longer. Give them a few logs for the night."

He left without a backward glance, back hunched, with little of the military about his bearing.

Thus, our transfer was postponed. A gendarme put some wood into the stove and left several more logs to see us through the night. He brought in a pitcher of water.

The girls asked permission to get some air, which was granted to them. A guard accompanied them.

"Nothing stupid now," he said, "or else . . ."

And he pointed to the revolver on his belt, laughing.

His colleague allowed me to stand in the doorway. He stood next to me, smoking his cigarette.

In front of me, very close, barbed wire, and over there, tragically close, with its twinkling lights, Geneva, salvation. One of my childhood regrets came flooding back: why didn't I have wings!

We went back in and resumed our place on the benches.

In halting sentences, the girls told how they had followed the guide to the level crossing when their group had suddenly found themselves face-to-face with two gendarmes and they had just enough time to see Julot taking off at full speed.

We tried to focus on our plight. But all we could say to each other was so pointless and gloomy that we ended up silent. The boy, who had been brought back after our search, had been asleep since dinner.

Fatigue soon got the better of the two girls: they fell asleep too, their sleep interrupted by sobs. The boy called out: "Mama!" and then his breathing grew regular once again, keeping time with the pacing of the German guard outside the customshouse.

I tried to put my thoughts in some sort of order and to think what last-ditch attempt might save me. The future appeared to offer little hope.

With my eyes fixed on the window bars, I listened to the muffled moaning of the wind.

As the miserly light of day started to break through, I was still awake, plunged deep in my miserable thoughts.

◇◇◇

At eight o'clock in the morning, the two gendarmes from the first team reappeared. It was Sunday, and they were in an excellent mood. It was as if they were telling us: "Now we've dealt with all the tedious bother you've caused us, we've nothing against you anymore."

Doubtless they were unaware of the exhaustion and suffering they had just inflicted upon us during their interminable interrogations, with no regard for our distress.

They did not appear to have any accurate understanding of the dreadful consequences that would follow our arrest. Turning cheerfully to one of the girls, one man said:

"Well, mademoiselle, it's not such a catastrophe to have to go to Germany to work! They pay well and they eat better than we do here."

Seeing my depressed state, another said to me:

"Come on, they won't force you to do any work that's too difficult. You're not twenty anymore! So, enough of that miserable face. Come on, come on!"

"They're all scared of working, these people we've been arresting for weeks," the first one resumed. "Do you think in Switzerland you get to eat without having to work?"

The girl with the intelligent expression tried to explain to him that, in our situation, the frightening problem was not working, but surviving: the Chancellor had vowed quite simply to exterminate the Jewish race.

I asked if either of them had been to a concentration camp for Jewish refugees. One gendarme related that, in fact, he had accompanied a convoy of one hundred fugitives and that on that occasion, he had had to spend a few hours at Gurs.

"And what did you see?" asked the girl.

"Oh, I saw some things, I did," he replied. "It's appalling the things that go on there! People go down like flies; old people, women, and children. Yes, I'll give you that! It's terrible, but they must have committed crimes or some sort of fraud in Germany. It seems they turned the country upside down before the war of 1914, and after 1918 they ruined Germany, taking all the wealth, all the gold, all the currency back to their Palestine, and to North and South America and a fair bit to Switzerland. So, you see! Now they're paying for it. A German Gauleiter officer 'esplained' it all to me [he said 'esplained']. And the Boches who come through here, they 'esplain' it too. We're not fond of them, the Germans, of course, 'cause what the hell are they doing here in our country, but well, as for the Jews, well, they've given the Boches a hard time, too. So you get it, don't you? We're just doing our duty, it comes from Vichy, from our government, these orders," he concluded with conviction.

The third, who had listened to this helpful explanation, added:

"As for me, I'd never seen any Jews before now. They're just people like anybody else. But the ones who come through here want to cross the border without even asking for a visa! So we pack them back off to where they come from. And they come back again. They're stubborn as mules. So we arrest them and put them in prison. It's given us all sorts of trouble for months. We've never had so much to do around here. You see, we don't care about the Jews . . . but they should stay where they are. The way they come to the border, they're keeping the whole police force busy, night and day. No offense, ladies, it's got nothing to do with you."

Such ignorance defied belief. I did not even try to set out the facts for them. I would have been just wasting my breath. "So, these men will continue to arrest hundreds of fugitives," I thought, "without ever understanding their role in the bigger picture, unless of course they just want to give themselves a moral alibi to assuage their consciences."

One gendarme, who had not participated in the conversation until then, appeared to have a better understanding of the issue, for he said sententiously:

"Be quiet, don't you realize we run the risk of being dismissed on the spot, or worse, if they hear us debating their decisions?"

And he gestured with his head in the direction of the German guard who was also carrying out "orders" as he trampled French soil.

At ten o'clock the boy was taken away to be sent back to the *département* of Creuse from whence he had come. A little later, a vehicle pulled up in front of the customs office. Some gendarmes "invited" us to collect our bags and climb in. And so we made the same journey back by car that we had made on foot the night before under Julot's disastrous guidance.

Passing by the ravine to which I had so strangely been drawn the previous night, and into which I had been ready to descend just moments before my arrest, I saw in the daylight that the strands of barbed wire were looser there. One of them was damaged, probably from a recent escape. I had been just a couple of steps from a possible way through! It would not have been too difficult to slip between the separated strands of wire. I was plunged into glum despair at this realization . . .

◇◇◇

We arrived at the Saint-Julien gendarmerie, where the police, having given our names to their colleagues and handed them our files, left us under their watch.

We were led into a makeshift cell which had a small window in its door. It was a former garage, divided into two sections. The first, near the entrance, was a sort of antechamber. The second was itself divided into two cells of equal size, each of which was able to be separately locked from the outside. On that day, the two cells were empty. In the corridor, an enameled container gave off a pestilential stench. Next to it, on a stone, stood a water jug.

Each cell had a pallet, mattresses stuffed with straw that had turned to dust, and military-issue blankets rolled into a bolster.

A girl accompanied by a gendarme brought us our midday meal, and while she was waiting to take away the basket and dishes, all three of us remained standing, not daring to sit down to eat on the revolting pallet.

Once we had finished, we asked permission to shake out our blankets in the courtyard and to sweep our prison cell.

The man replied that it was Sunday. But the girl, who had watched us eat with some pity, intervened on our behalf.

So, while the gendarme was chatting with her, we quickly set to work.

Under the same watch, we were permitted to wash at the end of a long corridor where there was running water from a fountain. Only when we were locked up again did we dare sit down on the little beds.

I begged our guard to be so merciful as to allow me to take a few steps outside. Feeling unwell and feverish, I was struggling to breathe. The young women followed me into the courtyard. After doing a few rounds under the pitying or indifferent looks of residents at their windows, we were taken back to our cell, which was double-locked by the gendarme.

We remained in darkness, utterly spent; the cold was biting. Finally we lay down on the filthy pallet. A little later, the door opened and the gendarme reappeared in the light of a lantern. He approached us and held out to me a parcel wrapped in newspapers.

"It's a hot brick," he said.

The parcel was burning hot. Touched by his thoughtfulness, we thanked him and held each other close, one against the other, sharing a bit of our warmth.

Broken by exhaustion and shock, I fell into a leaden sleep. When I awoke, an ashen-colored light was seeping through the little window. At my feet, the brick that had been so gratefully received was cold.

The door opened with a crash and our names were called. We were led over to a truck and made to climb in. We each received a ration of bread for the journey.

The vehicle was packed with fugitives who had been arrested in various places along the border and who, like us, were being transferred to Annecy.

XI

Annecy

After several hours traveling through spectacular mountains cloaked in their winter finery, the bus came to a town, passed through several streets, and stopped outside some high walls. A gendarme rang at a large iron gate, a lock creaked, a grille opened, and through we went to a yard inside the lockup.

We were in prison.

We were made to line up in a long corridor leading from the porch to several offices. The glacial wind swept through in all directions between the open doors. We were brought, one after another, before an officer who filled in our arrest warrants and made us complete and sign a questionnaire. Another officer took our fingerprints, carried out the usual measurements, and took our heights. We stood there, apathetic, holding our ink-blackened fingers apart, waiting patiently for these formalities to end.

The male detainees were then led to their section at the back of a large courtyard: there were twenty-eight of them. There were eleven of us women, including one with two small children. She was immediately transferred to the infirmary. Another had a six-year-old boy, who was entrusted to the care of an orphanage. The little one left without saying a word. He was exhausted, much like the adults.

At the officer's order, we followed a matronly woman who led us into another equally freezing room. There, she searched us meticulously, removing scissors, needles, and laces, and from me she confiscated a bottle of cough syrup. She couldn't know for certain what its contents were, she said. Once the bags had been put into storage, the warden went over to a closed door that had a peephole and bore the inscription: WORKSHOP, behind which could be heard a great humming of voices. She opened it and gestured to us to go in. The voices fell silent and all I saw at first, as if in a nightmare, were the pale faces of women turning toward us.

I remained for a moment near the doorway, leaning against the wall. My head was heavy and empty all at once. I examined the room. Two barred windows illuminated the white walls. The room was furnished with benches and three large tables. Opposite the door, another, smaller one was labeled in pencil: TOILETS.

As soon as the jailer had disappeared, the female prisoners all stood up and crowded around us, assailing us with questions. What news of the war? Had the persecutions increased or diminished in severity? Where had we come from? How had we been arrested? Where had it happened? And so on and so forth . . .

Lunchtime had long passed; as a result of our journey and the formalities of our registration, we had quite simply "skipped" it; the prisoners gathered together some provisions for us.

I sat down on a bench; I listened to the tales of escapes and arrests, all the while responding as best I could to the thousand questions prompted by my companions' anxiety. Every thought in that room revolved around these four issues: war, escape, arrest, deportation. This last word was uttered in a particular tone, the voice lowered a little, with a suppressed shiver and an expression of horror.

At six o'clock, the door opened and cast-iron pots containing vegetable, potato, and noodle soup were placed on the table.

"You new lot!" called out the jailer.

We presented ourselves before her, and we each received a mug and spoon. Knives and forks, possible instruments of suicide, were prohibited.

Half an hour later, censored letters and cards were distributed, followed by parcels, the contents of which were monitored. Most of the detainees' relatives had already been deported, so parcels were a windfall for a privileged few. The recipients recognized this and shared their offerings around.

At seven o'clock, the jailer reappeared to call out:

"Everybody to the dormitories!"

Then:

"You new lot!"

She handed us a sheet and a dark-gray towel. The lack of soap made doing the laundry impossible, so the prison simply had the linen boiled.

I followed the crowd of my companions in misfortune.

"Come and look," said one of them to me, "so you know what happens when your turn comes around."

In the corridor stood some galvanized metal containers. We carried them to the dormitories. We also brought with us a mug filled with water for the night. It took me several days of practice to become sufficiently skilled at this complicated carting to and fro.

The large dormitories each had twenty to thirty straw mattresses; the small ones three or four . . . I was put into one of the latter, which I shared with two detainees. We introduced ourselves.

One of my roommates was the mother of a famous singer in America. Her husband was incarcerated in the men's section. The couple were allowed to exchange two letters per week, and that poor woman lived for those scraps of paper, those so-called letters that she was meant to write in French and which she received in the same language. It wasn't easy, as the couple were Dutch and knew scarcely any French. We helped her as best we could with her correspondence.

The other woman, German, lively, and very pretty, was the wife of a onetime millionaire manufacturer who had managed to get part of his fortune out of Germany in 1935. The family had settled near Lyon. Her husband's professional contacts had quickly led to the establishment of a small but dedicated French clientele. In 1940, the law targeting German Jews led to their being sent to a concentration camp with their two daughters, after they were accused of being members of the Nazi Fifth Column in France. After months of effort, and thanks to the intervention in Vichy of a well-respected Lyonnais lawyer, the whole family was released.

Facing the imminent threat of deportation when the Germans arrived in Lyon, they were forced to flee to the Swiss border, from where they had been brought to the Annecy prison.

Even though these two couples had availed themselves of

the services of "first-class" smugglers, they had encountered the same fate I had, resulting in their imprisonment.

These two fugitives had set out in fur coats and elegant dresses with jewelry and a few small bags containing undergarments. They had not wanted to arrive in Switzerland in rags—at the time they had been convinced their attempt was likely to succeed.

I had employed the reverse technique with the same result.

What a peculiar spectacle they were, those two ladies, well groomed and elegant, sitting on their little iron bed in that cold, bare jail!

My two companions informed me that we had been remanded in pretrial detention. We would later have to undergo a formal trial. Its outcome would determine whether we would be released or transferred to one of the camps in France, from where we could probably expect to be deported. As a general rule, those under sixty who had committed the offense of traveling without a permit and with forged documents were transferred to the camps. I had to find myself a good lawyer as a matter of urgency. They had already done so.

I spent an uneasy, troubled night considering all these necessities. Much to my distress, I could not stop coughing. Of course, the dormitory was not heated and I had caught a chill walking toward Switzerland without any shoes.

◇◇◇

Six o'clock in the morning saw us making our "beds," for the jailer opened our doors at six-thirty to take us to the notorious "workshop."

There, two by two, we washed at the sink, which was served by two taps. The water was bitingly cold, but once we had washed, we were able to put on our coats and gloves once more and somehow we managed to warm ourselves up again. To this end, the women of German origin would do exercises.

The jailer reappeared, followed by two inmates who were serving sentences of two and three years, and announced:

"Attention, you lot! Coffee!"

We lined up, mugs in hand, and while one of the prisoners distributed the daily ration of bread, another poured us a drink of sorts. Then we remained in that same room, writing, reading, and trying to anticipate the future, all crowded in, one on top of the other. A broken pane of glass served as an open window.

Once a week, at around ten o'clock, the jailer announced:

"Attention, you lot! It's shopping time, ladies!"

We would then be allowed to write a list of the various authorized items we wanted brought in: writing paper, ink, penholders and pens (which always used to lose their nibs on their first use), soap made of sand and clay, and *sucrettes*, black lollies made of grape sugar, which were probably allowed in order to sweeten the bitterness of our days. And indeed, we did consume rather a lot of them.

Nobody here had any meal tickets. Ration cards found on fugitives were all confiscated, some belonging to French people and others being forged. Friends who had been informed of an arrest would often send cards to the prisoners. Members of the general public and French charities also brought cards to the prison management for our use.

The "workshop" was only a workshop in name. It was impossible to do any handiwork there for the simple reason that needles and scissors were prohibited. We idled our time away, interrupted every now and again by angry fights, for in addition to the thirty-five criminals of our kind "who had wanted to make a run for it without a permit," our company also included two professional thieves, convicted on three occasions, a fence, an accomplice to a forger of fake ration cards, and a girl of loose morals who had taken advantage of her "visit" to a hotel to make off with some clothes.

Relations between these women were far from harmonious, as they hurled the most colorful insults at each other. It was just as you'd imagine the "underworld" to be. I thought I was in one of Carco's novels about the Paris underworld . . .

Among the fugitives were a doctor from Alsace, a Polish pianist, two Belgian students, the wife of a rabbi from Antwerp, the wife of a diamond merchant from the same town, five Polish women with their children, a Russian woman from Baku, a Dutch woman, and numerous German and Austrian women.

Young or old, beautiful or ugly, fresh-featured or faded, young women or mothers, everybody had fled the prospect of deportation.

A smuggler volunteering her services—a young Frenchwoman who had led fugitives to the border—had been arrested and incarcerated with them. Kind and patient, she offered consolation to the weak. Her generous nature worked its influence on all the detainees who were continually asking her for advice and information.

Mademoiselle Adrienne was the only one of us who was always even-tempered.

When our jailer, whom we were supposed to call "*la patronne*" or "boss," came one morning to take several prisoners to the visiting room, I approached her and asked her to return my bottle of cough syrup.

She shouted:

"You've been told: no syrup!"

I tried to persuade her:

"I'm coughing and I'm keeping my roommates from sleeping."

At which she exploded:

"Is it me or you who's in charge here? How am I supposed to know what's in your bottle of syrup? Maybe you want to poison yourself! We've seen it all here! If you bring it up again, you'll be spending the night in the 'workshop.' Watch it, if I get angry, there'll be no letters and no parcels this evening for the lot of you," she growled as she left.

I was so intimidated by this attack that I went to hide behind my companions.

In an attempt to console myself, I wrote to the Mariuses, who would probably have heard about my misadventure from Monsieur Jean Letellier.

I soon realized our jailer was not so bad. Used to maintaining strict discipline among her customary inmates, our presence had thrown her into confusion. Disoriented, she concealed the discomfort we were causing her behind a loudmouthed, gruff severity.

Whenever we would turn to her and start with a:

"May I ask . . ."

She would interrupt immediately:

"There's nothing to ask. My job is to give orders. Obey them!"

We wouldn't dare then follow up with:

". . . for permission to close the window above the bed? We're being soaked by the rain."

Which wouldn't stop her from shouting the next day:

"How lazy can you be, leaving a window open so the rain pisses down on you!"

If, however, one dared to close a window without permission, she would exclaim in a hair-raising voice:

"Which one of you closed the window? Is it me who gives the orders here or you lot?"

We locked ourselves away in anxious silence.

"The boss has a mouth on her all right," said the fence. "She shouts so loud it's enough to give you a stomachache."

These scenes should have entertained us, but we were too rattled by the shocks we'd suffered. On the other hand, every day we would learn that some of our companions, upon leaving the prison, had been sent to Gurs. Tormented by the prospect of deportation, we were extremely nervous and took all of these daily incidents very seriously.

One Saturday evening, Mademoiselle Adrienne told us that Mass would be held at the prison chapel the following day.

"How about we all go and pray? God is there for everybody, regardless of any difference in religion," came the suggestion from one detainee.

Most of us agreed.

Before we were taken back to the dormitories, *la patronne* announced:

"Attention, you lot! It's Mass tomorrow! Which of you are coming?"

About twenty of us responded.

Taking great offense, she protested:

"If all the Jews who end up here these days turn up at the chapel, there won't be any room for decent Christian folk."

Gently, Mademoiselle Adrienne replied:

"Come now, madame, why stop these wretched souls from turning to God? Is that in the spirit of Our Lord?"

The reasoning confounded her. Words failed her. This time, she didn't even resort to her usual method of shrieking at the top of her voice! It was, I think, quite a memorable moment in her life.

But the next day she found her revenge. When the detainees came to enter the little chapel, up under the eaves of the prison building, she suddenly roared:

"Christians first!"

Perhaps this point of discrimination was made less out of authority than out of conviction. It was her individual way of demonstrating her Christian faith. It was clear our *patronne* did not have a dark soul, but was quite simply infatuated with the importance of her role as head jailer in the prison.

I mock our jailer now (whom we dared to call "Madame Attention-You-Lot . . ." in private) without any resentment and even with a hint of sympathy. Considering the unlimited power she wielded over us, it must be said she could have been even more of a dictator.

Our tormented, reclusive existence brought with it its moments of diversion. One Sunday, a beautiful Viennese woman, blond-haired, green-eyed, and elegant notwithstanding her advanced pregnancy, received a visit from her little son, who had been sent to an orphanage. The boy was accompanied by one of the nuns.

The sister told us that the gendarme charged with accompanying the child had asked him his name on the way there, in order to make sure he was delivered to the institution in an orderly fashion.

"What is your name?"

"François Besson," the child had replied, as he had been told to do by his parents (for the whole family had fake papers, as was customary).

"Yes, but what's your real name?"

"My name is François Besson," the lad had insisted adamantly.

When the gendarme tried to insist, the child, in no way put out, had ended up saying:

"Listen, if you don't believe me, ask Mama if it's true. I *know* my name is François Besson."

The gendarme was completely dumbfounded. What he didn't realize was that the moral resistance of this young son of Israel had been forged over dozens of centuries.

Next, the nun shared this story with us: the sister who looked after the children in the orphanage had asked the little boy:

"Is it your papa or mama who died?"

"I still have a papa and a mama, they're in prison, but you know, madame, they didn't steal anything. It's just because they're Jewish!"

And the good sisters were both stunned and moved to pity.

Feeling emboldened by his success, the boy told us in his delightful chatter that he had been given toys and that he was having fun with his little playmates.

"You know, Mama, they're not Jewish, but they're still nice. They don't beat me up."

The mother, proud as punch, told the women gathered around how her little boy had already stood up to the gendarmes when they were arrested. The young fellow interrupted her:

"I told them just what you taught me to, Mama."

He was a rosy-cheeked, fair-haired boy with a dimpled face,

just like his mother. Both his words and his attitude were unusually mature and considered. "One day," I thought, watching him, "he'll be one of those Jews who won't arouse any sympathy. People will think he's too shrewd, very knowing, and unbearably quick. After the education this life has handed him! Six years old! The poor little thing!"

The door to the "workshop" opened and *la patronne* announced:

"Attention, you lot! Time for soup!"

Pots of chickpea and noodle soup appeared on the tables, a Sunday treat.

Visiting time was over . . .

The gentle-natured nun from the orphanage and the pink-faced child left.

XII

Saint-Julien

At the end of a week, a group of prisoners was to be brought before the courts in Saint-Julien. Some were to be questioned by the investigating judge, others to appear before the Court of Assizes. I was among the first group.

At six in the morning, we were summoned by the traditional "Attention, you lot!" followed this time by an: "Off to court!" Then the *patronne* did the roll call, which she did her best to massacre; any attempt to correct her was met with:

"Sure, but what's the story with all these Turkish names? . . . I don't speak Latin."

And we laughed, and the *patronne* did too, proud and pleased with the pithiness of her own remarks.

We took our seats in the makeshift police van.

The trip to court provided us with a real diversion. It allowed us to leave the jailhouse for a few hours, to admire the sun, the forest, the fields, the Alps with their snowy peaks . . . winter in all its splendor.

This journey brought us into contact with more recent fugitives bearing news.

We traveled with other inmates: swindlers, vagrants, drunkards, burglars, and fences. The most significant character was a murderer, handcuffed and flanked by two gendarmes. He was sitting next to a beautiful brunette, who was accused of having danced in a public place. She called us as witnesses to the injustice inflicted upon her:

"Dancing! Is that a crime now?"

The men present expressed their outrage to make her happy.

Nobody mentioned that the only crime weighing on the conscience of most of the criminals in the wagon was having wanted to avoid deportation.

On arrival in Saint-Julien, we, the "new lot," had to appear in a little chamber before the investigating judge. He asked the usual questions and we set out the sole grounds that had forced us to risk fleeing. As we had not yet had any contact with a lawyer, "our case" was stood over for a week.

We were then brought into the large courtroom, where we were allowed to follow the proceedings.

First some criminal cases were heard.

To a man who had stolen ten chickens, the judge said:

"Granted, you wished to have a chicken to celebrate Christmas, but the other nine, why did you slit their throats, too?"

"It's just that, well, they came along all of their own accord, so to speak, so I thought of my mates. It's always nice to have a little chicken for Christmas."

He was perfectly serious. The witnesses testified to the fact that he had indeed shared the chickens around. The poultry exterminator was given a one-month suspended sentence.

Immediately thereafter came the day's most important matter: the murder trial. Experts gave lengthy evidence; witnesses were called. Then the accused—a tall, extremely pale man—rose.

Originally from Bremen, a German national, and Jewish, the murderer had sought refuge in France with his wife. They had initially led a peaceful existence in Paris, relying on funds sent by a Swiss relative. Then came the order to arrest all German Jews, collectively accused of being members of the Fifth Column. The couple found themselves separated: she was sent to Gurs, he to fortress detention. Six months later, the wife, suffering ill health, exhausted, her nerves completely shattered, was released. A month later, the husband was released pursuant to the amended law relating to German and Austrian Jews. They received a compulsory residence permit to live in a little village in the Alpes-Maritimes, where they resumed their everyday life.

However, the wife was unable to chase away the memory of the months spent in the Gurs camp, during which she believed her husband had been deported to the east. She made him swear to kill her if ever they found themselves in similar circumstances again. For a long time, the husband refused.

She suffered insomnia; one night, she swallowed the contents of a tube of sleeping tablets. They were able to revive her, but she immediately declared her intention to try again at the first opportunity. She was unable, she said, to continue living with the constant threat of deportation. In an attempt to reassure her, and not believing that the persecutions would resume, the husband had finally sworn to kill her and to follow her to her grave rather than let her be interned again. From that moment onward, she grew calm, almost serene. A nurse by profession, she started caring for the children and elderly of the village with such compassion and devotion that everybody showered the couple with sympathy and gratitude, as one witness testified.

The racist laws, first implemented in France in 1942, were now justifying increasingly violent persecutions. Like so many others, the couple resolved to make an ultimate attempt to escape to Switzerland.

Carrying only meager luggage, in which was hidden a large steel razor, they headed for the border with some other fugitives, led by a smuggler.

They were arrested just as they were about to cross the barbed wire. In a flash, while the gendarmes were busy with their companions, the woman pulled the razor out of her bag and, handing it to her husband, ordered him:

"Hans, you swore you would!"

Panicking too at their sudden arrest, the husband seized the murderous weapon and, as if hypnotized by the will of his wife, slashed her throat. The gendarmes dashed toward him, but he slashed himself deeply with the razor, twice, and fell down, bleeding, at his wife's side. His last movement, as reported by one of the customs officers, a witness to the scene, was to take the dying woman in his arms. This account was confirmed by another witness:

"I was there. That's exactly what happened!"

The doctor at the scene pronounced the woman dead and confirmed the desperate state of the man. He dressed the dying man's wounds and ordered his immediate transfer to the nearest hospital. The couple was brought to Z——, she to the morgue, he to an operating theater.

"How the murderer survived this injury is beyond me," the doctor reported to the bar. "I can testify, in all conscience, that it is a matter of pure chance and might even be viewed as a miracle if one recognizes the Divine at work here. What's more, one has only to look at the murderer's two dreadful scars to appreciate the extraordinary nature of the circumstances."

The doctor giving expert evidence then turned the prisoner's head and a shudder ran through the courtroom. The two large wounds, scarcely healed, were indeed visible, crisscrossed at the middle of his neck.

The doctor concluded:

"Having come to, the desperate man took advantage of a guard's momentary absence to tear off the bandage and was again found in a pool of blood. The hospital was thrown into confusion. Once more, one could say it was only the man's extraordinarily robust constitution that explains how he pulled through, against his will, for after this second attempt he had to be tied down."

The court was deeply moved.

It was then the prosecutor's turn to speak:

"Regardless of the tragic nature of this case, the fact remains: the wife was murdered; the husband is before you—alive. I ask for the usual sentence, taking into account the mitigating circumstances."

He resumed his seat and one sensed he had carried out his professional duty only very reluctantly.

The defendant's lawyer then set out the life story of the persecuted husband and wife, with its periods of hope each time dashed by surrounding events. He pleaded his case and closed with these words:

"Gentlemen of the jury, when the doctor here before you ordered the transfer of the dying man, who required an urgent operation, the ambulance went to the hospital in the nearest town, that of Z——. The mayor, who had been informed by telephone of the arrival of the vehicle's tragic cargo, made a decision which shall remain inscribed in shame: 'It's a Jew, I don't want any trouble with the Germans in my municipality, take him to Saint-Julien!' The convoy had to travel several kilometers further before being able to set down the dying man and the dead woman."

There was a shuffle of indignation among the jurors, which grew into a murmur of general condemnation.

"And that, gentlemen of the jury, is what happened in France in 1942! In order to put this abominable action to rights, I ask that this man, a man who cannot and must not be found guilty of murder, be released immediately, his only crime having been to have honored a sacred promise for which he'd intended to pay with his own life, there and then!"

An hour later, the defendant left the courtroom. Physically and emotionally exhausted, he was being supported by two charitable souls. He had been acquitted.

◇◇◇

The court was supposed to sit again in the afternoon, and as the inmates had to be taken back together, we were taken away until the end of proceedings to the "lockup," a place with which I was already familiar, having spent the night there prior to our incarceration in the jail.

This time, there were twenty-one of us, all crammed in, sitting and lying on the two pallets or standing in the corridor. Two pretty local Savoie girls brought us our meals from the neighboring farm. Cramped and falling over each other, but starving, we ate.

Over the hours of waiting, the captives told the stories of their odysseys, tales filled with poignant details: parents whose children had been taken away; mothers with no husband; a father with two young daughters of six and eight, the wife and mother having been torn away during a roundup at a market in Marseille. She had left to do the shopping and had not returned. A lawyer from Brussels, an industrialist from Mulhouse, a priest from Prague, dressed in peasant's garb; two German writers, a female doctor of psychoanalysis, also German, an Austrian opera singer, a rabbi from Antwerp whose family—seven of them—had been deported while he was leading a service, a pastor, a woman with her newborn, et cetera, et cetera. Each new "case" seemed more tragic than the last. A crescendo of suffering, deportations, and disappearances!

Of all of us, it seemed that Fate was smiling on the poultry exterminator. He was very pleased with the outcome of his trial and was enjoying our company. People shared their cigarettes and food with him; the poor chap appeared hardly to have eaten his fill since the famous Christmas Eve chicken feast.

Talking with those more recently arrested, we learned that the German authorities had replaced the Italian occupying troops with soldiers from the Reich throughout much of France; the Germans were winning everywhere, the political mood was with them, their diplomatic efforts were succeeding, and the occupied countries were straining under their increasingly heavy yoke.

◇◇◇

That evening, I heard my name called when the mail was being distributed: it was a letter from my dear professor, who had planned a stay in Nice but had instead settled in Lyon for family reasons. I had informed him of my arrest. He told me now that, given my circumstances (arrested for travel without a permit, attempted flight), the Gurs camp was unfortunately looking like a certainty; although, he added, without the imminent threat of deportation. He was promising to come and visit me as soon as I was transferred to that camp in order to discuss the possibility of securing my release.

All the kindness and loyalty demonstrated in his letter could not console me in the face of the prospect of being sent to Gurs. I spent a troubled night looking for a way out and pondering the possibilities of a new attempt to escape. There were none I could see. The thought of taking the ultimate way out briefly crossed my mind. Three days earlier, just as she had been about to be transferred, a woman had cut her veins by breaking a windowpane in the room where she had been locked up to wait for the gendarmes. I was keenly aware that I lacked this sort of courage. Too many ties still bound me to this world; I loved life, and the thought of seeing my mother and relatives again gave me the strength to try to save myself.

The following day, when the mail came, my name was again read out. It was a letter from the Mariuses. They wrote to say how sorry they were for me, what an anxious time Christmas had been, and they spoke of the friends who constantly came to them asking for news of me. They asked, with sympathy, after my fate: incarceration or camp? And how might they reach me?

The money I had asked for had been sent to my lawyer by telegraph. They also wrote that they had sent ration cards, via the same delivery as my letter, to the prison management. This letter encouraged and comforted me; I now knew I could rely on the support of a lawyer, the ultimate hope of every detainee.

Two days later, a parcel arrived, containing such an array of marvels and rare treats that it caused a sensation: two rabbit legs, glacé fruits, soap, two towels, and a bedsheet.

The inmate who was an accomplice to the forger of fake ration cards said:

"But that's a real piece of real soap!"

I also discovered three needles hidden in a box, underneath a ripe Camembert. For the first time in a long time, I rediscovered the pleasures of the palate, for the task of eating had become a form of dismal duty.

That night, Cinderella slept on a white sheet, her makeshift pillow covered with a clean towel.

◊◊◊

One morning, the *patronne* summoned me in a stentorian voice. I followed her into the visiting room, where my lawyer was waiting for me, and we introduced ourselves.

In addition to the telegraphic transfer, he had also received my passport and various documents. The famous 1939 reference from the office of the President of the Council made another appearance! The Jules Chancel volume also featured in the file.

The lawyer was very affable as we discussed matters. He told me, smiling, that my file contained documents capable of clearing me of much more serious crimes than an attempted escape to Switzerland. Furthermore, he said to me, the severity of the legal system had relaxed a little, with the attention of the German authorities recently focused elsewhere. Some refugees had been released once they had served their sentence, others had been sent back to their former places of residence or sent on to parts of the country under less strict Nazi control. The current trials, he explained to me by way of clarification, were nothing more than a necessary formality, in the absence of which the Germans would quickly, and at the first excuse, take on all such responsibilities themselves, involving themselves in the courts, and ultimately handling the country's entire law-enforcement and judicial systems. Thus, it was necessary to maintain an appearance of strict severity toward the refugees so as not to offer any pretext for them to seize control of France's institutions.

The week was starting auspiciously, affording me some hope to which I clung optimistically.

That week was also marked by the release of Mademoiselle Adrienne, who, before she left, offered each of us a word of encouragement, or some advice. She gave me the addresses of several people whom I could call on for help and guidance once I had regained my freedom.

Other detainees leaving the jail promised to send us news to keep us informed of their fate and thereby prepare us for what, in turn, awaited us.

The week finished with a noteworthy revelation: during our collective time in the "lockup" several of us had acquired body lice. It caused quite a stir! We embarked on a process of feverish and diligent mutual delousing that took an entire day. I felt as if I were in one of those vast monkey enclosures where it had so amused me in my youth to watch the monkeys engaged in the same task.

◇◇◇

Once again, the *patronne* came in and, in a particularly strict, serious tone, announced:

"Attention, you lot! Off to court."

Then followed the detainees (who, in the meantime, had become "old-timers"), whose names she now pronounced with absolute assurance and an impeccable accent, and then the names of the "new lot," who were, in turn, required to appear before the investigating judge.

With a private quiver of joy, the prisoners, male and female, climbed into the prison van.

On the way there, our vehicle collided with a truck. After the crash, the motor refused to start again; it was as if a giant's heart had stopped beating at the shock of its own crime. Its victim, the truck, was lying crushed in the ditch next to the road. The driver tried hard to revive the beast, aided by some gendarmes, but in vain. The detainees were forced to complete the journey of several kilometers on foot. There were quite a few of us, and the group walking the slowest, who were "lagging behind espressly on purpose," as one of our guards maintained, were handcuffed.

Lockup, fingerprints, appearance before the magistrate's court, handcuffs, nothing was missing from this picture. When we entered the courtroom, heavily guarded by our escort of gendarmes, I was reminded of an illustration from an edition of one of Georges Courteline's novels. The likeness brought a smile to my face.

The first case to be heard involved a people smuggler who, for months, had led numerous escapes at prices of up to one hundred thousand francs a head. He was sentenced to three years' hard labor by reason of the exorbitant sums he had charged.

Then it was the turn of a woman carrying an infant in her arms. She received a sentence of one month's detention for having attempted to flee. She was also being called as a witness to give evidence against her smuggler.

After getting his hands on the agreed sum, the smuggler had demanded five more thousand-franc notes from her once they were under way.

"I know you have more money on you," he had said to her.

"I won't deny it," the woman responded, "but I don't know anybody in Switzerland and, as you can see, I have a sick baby."

"If that's how you want to play it," he had replied, "I'm ditching you."

So the woman had complied with his request. A little more than a mile further on, the infant cried, a gendarme appeared, and the smuggler took off.

She was transferred to the customshouse where, not without some pleasure, she discovered that the crook had been arrested shortly after her.

The prosecutor and judges admonished the accused sharply. He was found guilty of fraud and blackmail.

Then four young people aged between twenty-two and twenty-five appeared. Just as war was declared, they had been working as volunteers with a group of fifty young Polish Jewish people. After the armistice, they had been sent to Morocco and made to do "national service" in the Foreign Legion. About fifteen of them, however, who had family in France, were permitted to remain in camps in mainland France and were later released. Then came the persecutions, and eight of those doing "national service" were deported to Germany. Some of the others miraculously managed to reach England. The last four had covered the distance between the Alpes-Maritimes and the Swiss border on foot, only to end up . . . before the magistrate. They had served their time while remanded in custody awaiting trial. The judges conferred and concluded that the four former volunteers would be in less danger in a French labor camp than being supposedly "free."

A diamond merchant from Antwerp, whose wife had died in a Belgian camp and whose five children were scattered all over the place, appeared, like the majority of us, on a charge of traveling with forged papers and unlawful attempted flight. For his part, he was bringing a counterclaim against the militiamen who had arrested him.

"When he was searched," his lawyer was explaining, "two little silk bags containing diamonds had been found on his person, sewn into the lining of his overcoat. Attached to each little bag was an itemized list indicating the weight, color, and dimensions of each stone. The diamond dealer had sewn a copy of that list into his cap and had left a third copy with French friends in Grenoble. In the event of any misfortune befalling him, his friends had promised to claim the diamonds; they were planning on returning the precious stones to his children, should they ever reappear. When the two little bags were discovered, the soldiers confiscated them and left. When they returned, some of the stones were missing and the list had disappeared. The diamond dealer refused to countersign the statement pertaining to the seizure. Knowing he was lost and having nothing to fear, he wanted, at the very least, to save that part of his fortune for his children."

The officers ended up admitting they had taken the two little bags into another room.

"There was such a crowd in there that it was impossible for us to examine such small items in peace. The detainee is only accusing us to seek revenge," declared one of them.

Arguing that removal of the arrested man's property was unlawful, his lawyer asked the court to uphold his client's claim. The trial was postponed for a fortnight while the necessary searches were conducted.

Three elderly ladies with startlingly bright white hair appeared before the court at the same time, defended by the same lawyer. The youngest of them was . . . sixty-two years old, the eldest seventy-two. The tallest woman stood between the other two, who were slighter, almost fragile. They appeared together, all for the same offenses: travel without a permit, forged papers, attempted flight.

One of them had a married daughter in Zurich; the other, deprived of her son, who had been deported by the Germans, had wanted to accompany her friend. The third had been forced to leave the Jewish community's retirement home in Toulouse, which had been closed by order of the Vichy government, and she had quite simply found herself without a roof over her head. She had set off for Switzerland, a country she had been assured would be a safe haven for such unfortunate souls.

Looking at those three old women, I wondered how they had imagined being able to cross the barbed wire! Had they considered the difficulties they would encounter? Or were they simply unaware of them? Or did they think that, since the Red Sea had parted to allow the children of Israel to pass, the strands of barbed wire would also separate to allow passage for the likes of such poor old women seeking their freedom? Did they still believe in the miracles that featured so prominently in their ancestors' stories? Had they forgotten that, since those long-gone times, their God, the Eternal, God of lightning and vengeance, appeared to have well and truly abandoned His chosen people?

After a touching scene, all three of them were acquitted with an order to return to their former places of residence.*

Then, as if in a dream, I heard my name called. I rose; I felt, rather than saw, the judges turn to look at me. I remained standing while my lawyer stated my offense: attempted escape, but in possession of a Swiss visa. While such cases generally involved foreigners who had recently come to France to flee persecution, I had lived in this country for a long time, and studied here. He recounted how I had been hounded, and forced to go into hiding for months. He stressed the fact that Swiss friends, informed of my plight, had sent me an entry visa. Compelled to take action by the dangerous circumstances, and very reluctantly, I had ultimately tried to leave France, the country I considered to be my second homeland. This attempt to flee with forged papers which, out of consideration for the Frenchwoman who had lent them to me, I had prematurely returned, had failed.

"Had she retained those papers, my client could easily have passed for a Frenchwoman and turned back."

Raising his voice, the lawyer then read out the 1939 letter of reference. At the passage *"May she avail herself of every freedom and benefit our nation has to offer,"* a murmur rose among the judges.

That reference, rebuffed, disregarded, scorned even, on so many occasions, now allowed my lawyer to ask for special per-

---

* In February 1944, friends wrote to tell me that one of these dear old ladies, after whom I regularly inquired, had been arrested by the Gestapo and transferred to the camp at Drancy.

mission to be granted, allowing me to reside in any village or town of Haute-Savoie, including in Annecy, as well as for the right to move freely within the limits of that *département*.

My defense counsel's application was upheld in its entirety. I was given the minimum suspended sentence and pronounced free.

I was brought back to the jailhouse in Annecy, where I had to wait until the following day for the release formalities to be completed.

For the first time in a very long time, I slept soundly, free of nightmares and anxiety.

We went down to the "workshop" as usual at six-thirty in the morning. This time, I was carrying my bundle of possessions, my sheet and my towel, for I was hoping never to have to return to that dormitory.

I was hoping, but without too much conviction . . .

XIII

Annecy

At the clerk's office, I was handed back my two pieces of jewelry and my money. *La patronne* returned the items that had been left in storage. She was almost affable with me now, while maintaining the necessary distance, of course. She persisted with her hostility toward the cough syrup right up until my departure. When she handed it back to me, visibly reluctant, I thought I might make light of it. I took the stopper out of the bottle and swallowed a few mouthfuls. She gesticulated in fright. So, the warder really was convinced it was some sort of poison!

"Enough! Enough! I wouldn't like to see you croak within the prison walls," she said, severely.

I never did understand why she had been so suspicious of that pink syrup.

At around ten o'clock, a member of the French Militia came to fetch us to take us back to the police station, where our lawyers would hand us the orders for our release. There were eight of us leaving the jail: five women and three men.

Finally, a heavy gate opened to allow us to leave. How joyful we were, walking with a spring in our step. The prison guard shouted: "One, two! One, two! Get a move on!," evidently wanting to exercise his power one last time.

Before turning the corner of that memorable street, I took one last look at the tall building with its high walls, the bare branches of a miserable tree poking out over the top. I had often contemplated that tree: it had continued to grow upward in its nostalgic quest for space and freedom.

"At four o'clock we'll be heading to Gurs!" came the sudden announcement from the militiaman.

"To Gurs? . . . To Gurs?" cried eight voices at the same time. "But haven't our lawyers confirmed we're free to go?"

"No," the man replied, abruptly, "in accordance with a new decree dated yesterday, everybody is to be transferred to Gurs!"

It was entirely possible. A leaden grief settled over us. We entered the police station, despairing.

An hour later, three lawyers appeared, produced release orders, and left with their clients.

◇◇◇

My lawyer had not come and I found myself suddenly alone. I was in such a state that I felt as though I was going mad.

The militiaman kept throwing sneering looks in my direction. I overcame my abiding sense of loathing and asked him to please telephone my lawyer to remind him of my situation. He refused outright, saying it was not the job of the gendarmes to run around after release orders, quite the contrary!

"The lawyers will just have to come here, that's what they're paid for, damn it!"

Then he left, thank heavens.

Soon afterward, a gendarme came in and reassured me. He was perfectly aware my name was on the list of those to be released, he said.

"Forget whatever that *other* fellow said," he added, "he likes a joke. Everything will be fine. Just be patient!"

But I couldn't anymore. Utterly exhausted and beside myself, I burst into tears.

Seeing me shaken by sobs, my guard dashed off to look for a glass of cold water, which he offered to me, saying, "There, there!" over and over in a paternal fashion.

Shortly after midday, my lawyer, who had been held up before the court in the morning, called the police station to say he was bringing my release order that afternoon. The gendarme seemed completely delighted at the news. He handed me some papers to sign and said:

"You're free. I knew you would be. And now, go and have a decent meal and a nice glass of wine."

Moved, I held out my hand to him:

"Thank you, monsieur, you are a true Frenchman!"

He took my fingers, squeezed them vigorously, and suddenly serious said:

"Courage, madame! They'll pay for all this, I swear, so long as I call myself a Savoyard!"

And with that, he had made the same solemn oath as Monsieur Marius, that man of the Midi.

◇◇◇

With unsteady steps, I crossed the vast courtyard. I couldn't help but turn around every second moment to make certain I wasn't being followed by a gendarme. Seeing that there really wasn't anybody behind me, I left without hurrying. I suddenly felt so light-headed I had to sit down on a stone bollard at the entrance. I closed my eyes, my bundle of possessions at my feet, and tried to settle my breathing.

The square in front of me seemed enormous. I didn't have the courage to cross that vast expanse. So, when an elderly lady approached, I spoke to her:

"Please, madame, allow me to walk next to you, just to the nearest restaurant."

She helped me to my feet, picked up my bundle, and, taking me by the arm, led me as if I were an invalid. I shall never forget her gentle, affectionate support. She did not ask me a single question. How grateful I was to her for that!

Slowly, she guided me to a table at a glassed-in terrace. I thanked her warmly.

After greeting the owner, with whom she appeared to be on very good terms, she gestured to me in friendly farewell as she left.

A delightful brunette, the daughter of the house, as I was subsequently to discover, came to serve me. I asked if she would be so kind as to put in a telephone call to the Mariuses.

She told me foreigners were not permitted to make outside calls, but offered to carry out the necessary formalities on my behalf.

I started to eat, gazing out to the lake, the sun, the sky, the trees, and the people passing by.

An hour later the connection was put through: the Mariuses were on the line. They told me how delighted they were to know I had been released, promising they would come to see me in Savoie. Our conversation ended in peals of laughter with a peculiar acoustic phenomenon making our words echo. Was someone listening in on our call? I don't know. We paid no attention: I was free!

I stayed there in the sun a long time, reading, writing letters, taking in everything around me: the countryside, the passersby, the comings and goings on the street. I was reconnecting with everyday life . . . When I wanted to pay for my telephone call and my meal, I learned, to my great embarrassment, that my lunch had been paid for by the kind lady who had accompanied me, and that I was welcome to another coffee and dessert, both of which had also been covered. This display of sympathy, the young Savoyard woman's kindness, and the Mariuses' encouraging words went a good way to restoring my courage.

Out on the street, I experienced a sort of vertigo which, for more than a week, would come on every time I ventured outside.

◇◇◇

At the corner of Rue Royale, I ran into the pretty Viennese woman and her precocious son. Given her advanced pregnancy, she had been released and allowed to stay in a local hotel while awaiting the trial of her husband and father, both of whom were in prison, but she was under surveillance, meaning she had to report to the police station twice a day.

We chatted. She advised me to go to her hotel; the owners, she said, were decent Savoyards who looked kindly on refugees.

That was, indeed, a useful recommendation and I made my way there without delay.

It was only six in the evening, but exhaustion and, most of all, the appeal of a bed with white sheets, an actual bolster, a real duvet, and even two blankets . . . was irresistible, and I lay down. The maid brought me two hot water bottles and, fifteen minutes later, a milky tea and some bread and cheese on a tray! I tried all of these "delicacies," then, like an exhausted animal, I abandoned myself to the exquisite pleasure of sleep.

Days went by. I couldn't quite manage to recover my peace of mind. Heavy steps in the stairwell, the bell ringing in the middle of the night, loud voices on the landing all made me sit bolt upright, covered in sweat and short of breath.

◇◇◇

One night, three violent blows were heard at the neighboring door.

"Who's there?" shouted a male voice.

"Police!" came the harsh reply.

The door opened after several minutes and I heard my neighbor exclaim:

"You fool! Are you mad? What are you doing waking me up like that?"

To which the visitor replied with a laugh:

"Looks like I gave you a fright. It's just a joke!"

"Funny joke!" grumbled the other man. "And just when the police are clamping down all over the place."

They then started chatting about other things.

And there I was, all dressed, my Annecy resident's permit in one hand, and in the other my little suitcase. How was it that I had managed to ready myself in the space of a few minutes? After the roundups in Nice, I had grown extremely skilled at this sort of thing . . .

The following day, all the hotel residents were talking about the "nocturnal joke." Those who had been released, and, even more so, those in hiding preparing to flee, had been thrown into a panic. The practical joker had been neither callous nor malicious, he had simply failed to understand the atmosphere of the times.

I smile now at the memory of my panic and, most of all, at how I must have looked at that moment . . .

While in Annecy, I caught up with most of the detainees who had been released. They were all waiting for travel permits in order to return to their former places of residence.

But now the postcards and letters we were receiving from other parts of France once again put us on alert.

One Austrian woman informed us that hardly had she been released and had returned to the Alpes-Maritimes when she suddenly became "gravely ill" (code for being in danger of being deported), and Sophie (as she was calling herself) had "once again set off" toward Grenoble, evidently to be near the border again.

Another woman told us of a serious "attack of rheumatism" (need to escape).

A German woman, who had left the jail with her husband and returned to their home in Nîmes, learned once there that "the François" (militiamen) had come by "to invite them over"; the couple were now living on a big farm where "they were being cared for" (hidden) while waiting for "the grapes to be harvested" (to make a new attempt to escape). In Haute-Garonne, there had been an outbreak of "scarlet fever" (deportations).

We found out from two young women in Gurs that "their father" (their lawyer) had not given up hope of seeing them again soon, and that "the weather conditions were currently favorable for hiking in the mountains." Many informed us also that their families had been deported.

But in the Isère, "the weather was superb, almost like spring," and the poor souls there, it seemed, were regaining a taste for life.

Those inmates who had obtained temporary permits to stay in various small towns in Savoie were likewise optimistic about what the future held. This respite, which felt like a holiday, had calmed spirits and revived people's courage.

◇◇◇

In Nice, Grenoble, and in my encounters with other fugitives, I had often heard mentioned the name Father F——, from Annecy.

Like so many distraught refugees seeking assistance and comfort, I found my way to him upon my release. The house was deserted. I knocked at a door at the end of a corridor.

The priest came to open it himself. He was standing against the light and I could only make out his tall silhouette. He took me into a large room full of books, and bade me sit down at a table laden with papers and packages of every size. Some were not tied up and I spotted coffee, rice, sugar, tea . . . Every chair was covered in larger parcels, and in order to sit down himself, the priest had to lift one of them off. He sat down at his desk opposite me and only then did I see him in the full light of day.

His face, his features, wore a look of infinite peace. Never have I seen such an open expression. You immediately felt that he trusted you. He radiated goodness and his presence was as reassuring as a beautiful sunny morning on a peacetime day.

Father F—— must have considered me to be in a bad way, for he came the very next day to tell me that the Mother Superior of a convent was offering to take me in while I gathered strength and regained my peace of mind.

I willingly accepted the invitation and took myself off to the convent, which stood out white against the backdrop of the mountains.

When I pulled on the bell, an invisible hand seemed to push the gate, which opened onto a beautiful garden full of fruit trees.

I approached the entrance.

Sister Ange had played the role of gatekeeper for thirty-five years. How many human beings must have entered the convent under her benevolent gaze over that long period of time!

Her face had become the very manifestation of welcome after taking so many people in. She appeared to have been told of my circumstances and invited me to make myself comfortable in the room near the entrance, while I waited to be summoned by "our Mother."

We were sitting by the window. Sister Ange was telling me about the trees, one of the great earthly pleasures of the good sisters, who devoted themselves to gardening. She gave me a beautiful winter apple harvested from their crop; it was a species, she told me, found only in Savoie, and they were especially delicious that year.

You could hear children singing and laughing: an orphanage was attached to the convent.

The Mother Superior greeted me with kindness. She told me the convent was caring for several children, orphans whose parents had been deported. They were to be taken to Switzerland by a Carmelite sister any day now.

"They never laugh," she sighed.

For months and months now, so many miserable, hunted souls had found a moment's respite at the convent.

The Mother Superior lifted her gaze to the ivory Christ and was silent. She was praying.

I was moved by this motherly welcome and made my way toward the rear of the building feeling greatly comforted.

◇◇◇

Nothing broke the silence of the convent. The garden, completely white, sheltered me from the outside world. The mountains formed a second protective circle around me. Peace reigned throughout.

Slowly I resumed life's rhythms.

In the morning, at six o'clock, a bell vigorously announced it was time to wake up.

You could hardly hear the muffled steps of the sisters leaving the light-filled sleeping quarters.

Not long afterward, the bell called them to the chapel, soon followed by the crystalline sound of the little bell during Mass.

The sun would rise in all its glory and bathe the silent convent, the mountains, the entire world, in light.

After Mass, the sisters would head off to perform their humble tasks and daily duties with visible serenity.

Sister Célestine would tell the children stories of pagans and infidels, of corrupted and diabolical souls who had, in the fullness of time, been granted heavenly grace. Her faith in the power of miracles was profound and infectious. Her audience listened to her eagerly, spellbound.

The surrounding countryside was calming, though it could

not provide me with the same solace it had once offered. I knew it was only a respite. I took advantage of those days of fleeting peace as one swallows a precious remedy, gulped down to restore one's strength ahead of battles to come.

War continued to rage in Europe, increasingly bloody, as were the persecutions.

And my relatives were in another part of the world, unreachable.

The past was still recent and the future remained full of threat.

We would run into Father F—— every day. Sometimes he would be making his way down a hill on his bicycle, his cassock bearing traces of his challenging rounds.

He visited the sick and infirm throughout the countryside, consoling the despairing, and would go so far as to push through the scrubby undergrowth of the maquis, delivering letters, supplies, cigarettes, and encouragement to French civilians refusing to be drafted to work for the Germans.

Sometimes, when I went to see him at the presbytery, he was just about to head out. I would see him fill the pockets of his cassock with the most diverse items: a bottle of medicine, packets of cigarettes, a quarter of a kilogram of coffee, two pairs of socks, a shirt, and one day, even, a quart of red wine!

Seeing my astonishment, he joked:

"You wouldn't believe what you can fit into a priest's pockets, would you? Wait! I almost forgot . . ."

And he added a pair of slippers, which, indeed, he still managed to fit in!

He laughed heartily.

He would often come to ask after me at the convent, the ideal retreat to which he had brought me just as my resistance was failing.

Sometimes he would talk to me about his parishioners—the sick, a baptism, somebody dying—and always with the same care and affection.

He never overlooked anybody, and would openly receive fugitives, setting them on the path to the border himself or entrusting them to the care of country folk who took on that perilous task without hesitation. He could always find French people ready to help the persecuted, and houses in which to shelter them.

He was neither cautious nor measured in the performance of his charitable works, throwing himself boldly, head held high, into the danger he must have known existed.

Did he believe, in his profound faith, that Providence would not desert him in the fulfillment of his Christian duty? Or was he quite simply embracing his fate, placing himself in God's hands and humbly accepting His decisions in advance?

◇◇◇

One morning, I was unable to get up. The illness that had lain dormant within me for a long time now made itself known with a vengeance. Burning with fever, I remained in a state of semiconsciousness for ten days.

Like a distant vision, the white wings of Sister Ange's wimple loomed over me. I drank a variety of cooling, fragrant herbal infusions that quenched my thirst and seemed like refreshments from Heaven itself.

I had been overcome by a great need to sleep. And so I slept. I dreamed I was in an abyss shimmering with opalescent, sleep-inducing vapors, and it was pointless to resist. I abandoned myself to its powers.

Sometimes, I would also dream I had fallen asleep for the last time. I was filled with an overwhelming sense of peace. I was tormented by just one regret, that I would not see my dear elderly *maman* again. And so I wept, calling out in my delirium.

When I came to once more, April was smiling weakly beyond the windows of my room.

The leaves on the trees were starting to come out.

The sky was a pale blue.

Spring was blossoming.

Madame Marius came to visit me. She was welcomed into the convent. She brought me a visa that had been renewed by the Swiss Consulate in Nice and told me that most of our acquaintances had been deported; the others were in hiding. The Italians had been powerless for a long time now. The Germans had replaced them everywhere in the Alpes-Maritimes . . .

She expressed her fears for me. I mustn't wait any longer.

When Madame Marius left again for Nice, we said goodbye to each other for the remainder of the war.

XIV

At the border

O n a magnificent spring day in April, I set off for the border for the second time.

I had been given very precise directions to a spot where the barbed wire was not very high, since a water-filled ditch served as a natural obstacle. One could get across there, the only risk being that of catching a bad cold, easier to cure than deportation to Germany!

In those times, the possibility of catching a cold was, indeed, only a laughable risk...

Thus, I made my way toward the ditch that day with a light step, walking alongside the barbed wire, just beyond which, within arm's reach lay... Switzerland!

On more than one occasion I was tempted to clamber over the metal strands without wasting another moment, and jump to the other side. But it would not have been easy and my instructions were clear: wait until I came to the ditch!

At last, I reached it . . .

Hitching my dress up, I prepared to cross it.

"What are you doing?"

I had been seen by a soldier who suddenly sprang out from behind the tree where he had been hiding.

I realized it would be pointless to reply and, furthermore, I would not have been capable of uttering a single word.

I knew this second attempt would be classed as a repeat offense and would lead me straight to Gurs without trial. I knew everything that awaited me and yet all I felt was an emptiness, an absence. I felt removed from everything. Time seemed to have stopped in its tracks.

An eternity went by.

"We're going back to Saint-Julien," I heard a voice declare in the singsong tones of Italy.

We set off. My mind was empty.

After a couple miles, two Mobile Guards riding bicycles appeared on the road.

I felt a dreadful sense of horror. At the same time, the soldier took me by the arm.

The guards approached.

Suddenly, the soldier started talking to me:

"*Bel tempo!* Sun! Good for the soil! Me, farmer, down there. *Terra napolitana. Bella, bellissima terra!*"

The guards passed by.

In Saint-Julien, the Italian stopped at the buses. He told me to board the one that was leaving for Annecy, made sure I was settled, and left my bundle on my knees. He had taken it from me and carried it the whole way.

He got off again and the bus departed.

A Neapolitan peasant had just given me the gift of life—he had not turned me in . . .

And as I admired the grandiose views of the Alps unfolding before me, I could hear once again the sweet song of gratitude swelling within me . . .

◇◇◇

I headed back to Annecy and returned to the hotel, where I received a very warm welcome from the owner. She handed me a notice summoning me to the prefecture of police: it informed me that my extended residence permit was to be withdrawn.

The Viennese woman was still living there with her "two men," as she called her father and husband. She brought me up to date with recent developments: the situation had deteriorated significantly.

All refugees, she told me, without exception, were being forced to appear at the police station twice a day, by recent order of the Vichy government; people were pouring in from the *départements* where deportations were rife and escapes to Switzerland were again as common as they had been in December.

At the prefecture I joined a line of foreigners being grilled as to their identity by an official, who was not, however, insisting overly on questions of race. Those whose race had not yet been stamped on their documents received a residence permit that did not mention it, an omission that would prove very significant in the coming days!

I felt safe for a few more weeks, even though danger still lurked in the shadows.

There were more and more cars about, filled with Germans. They took up residence in a large hotel in town; it was said they were members of the Gestapo. They had set up a recruitment office for French labor in the middle of Rue Royale, where buses filled with young men would pull up. Sometimes there would be demonstrations around the buses, and the laborers within—prisoners, in effect—would escape with the help of passersby.

The front windows of the office displayed various caricatures of blatant anti-Semitic propaganda.

But to the outside world, the *département* appeared to be under the peaceful rule of the Italian Occupation.

Upon my return, I had all the time in the world to stroll around Annecy and I made some very curious finds.

A water fountain murmuring in the middle of a square. Nearby, a little bridge from ancient times, looking toylike with its delicate balustrade.

A footbridge seemingly lifted straight out of a theater set; the lively rushing stream and pervasive smell of watery plant life the only things to remind you that it was real. On the street corner, an old church surrounded by dilapidated buildings.

In the next street, a decrepit, damp tower with narrow windows: a former prison. It held inmates until just a few years ago. Now it has fallen into disuse. How fortunate!

I lose my way in the alleys, walking down a long, dark passage beneath ancient homes; I feel a shiver down my spine. Suddenly, I emerge onto the sunny square of another church. In another laneway, an electric lamp seems such an anachronism in this me-

dieval place. Its light flickers under a thousand-year-old arch. Old
steps spiral upward. Up we go. They smell musty. But it is not
to any sinister abode they lead; standing outside an intricately
carved oak door, I wonder, shall we use this bronze knocker? In
we go . . . the house resembles a museum!

Time has been kind to the pale colors on the ceiling; the
floor is a veritable mosaic of marquetry. There are paintings on
the wall, and in the display cabinets old porcelain, and lacework,
which is older still.

I resume my promenade through Annecy: look! An ancient
gate with iron lacework in blooms of intertwining flowers; an old
portal flanked with bas-reliefs of characters from the Scriptures.

So many little shops in the town's old quarter have carved or
brightly painted wooden signs.

One can't help but be enthralled by the architectural purity
of the grand old houses.

The house of François de Sales is still alive with the glorious
past of that enlightened, saintly, and aristocratic spirit.

Now I find myself in the garden of the former Bishop's Palace, with its beautiful lawn. I stop to gaze at a thousand-year-old
acacia, with its array of white flowers. Its neighbor, a pink acacia,
stands opposite. Two old friends, the same age as each other; the
ground is covered by the iridescent carpet of their mixed petals,
as is the still surface of a little stream that leads nowhere.

I sit down on a mossy bench, in the shade of a sturdy oak tree,
and watch the children of France gracefully dancing in a circle
and singing:

> *Nous n'irons plus aux bois,*
> *Les lauriers sont coupés . . .*

We'll to the woods no more,
The laurels have been cut . . .

◇◇◇

All the while, events were running their course.

My second visa had by now expired too.

Monsieur Marius, who knew of my failed second attempt to flee, had gone to the consulate in Nice and learned that my permit, renewed for the third time, could be collected from the consulate in Annemasse.

At the same time, I was informed by my Swiss friends that they had obtained one last extension and that henceforth it would be impossible for them to make any further requests.

From one day to the next, then, I found myself faced with this distressing dilemma: either to run the risk of no longer having a visa or to risk a third attempt to flee.

In the middle of all this, and without any warning, Monsieur Marius appeared. He had taken forty-eight hours' leave to travel for thirty-four hours, which he considered his duty toward me.

He told me of the horrifying events unfolding in the Alpes-Maritimes since my departure from Nice and said:

"I am a man of no formal education nor learning . . . forgive my presumptuousness: but I tell you, it is futile and dangerous to wait. Better to make another attempt to escape than to remain under such rule. Oh! How dreadful it all is! The things I have seen! I have only one thing to say: leave, madame!"

I gave him a guided tour of the best Annecy had to offer.

He found the town very small and the lake very beautiful, "but it wasn't the sea."

He sent off half a dozen postcards to relatives and friends

in Nice. He had a laugh thinking of their astonishment upon hearing of his extraordinary escapade: it was the first trip of his working life!

He quickly felt terribly homesick for his wife, his lively business, and most of all, for Nice's sunshine!

"You can say what you like," he repeated, "it's not the same sun as ours back home!"

Upon his return to Nice, he sent me a card telling me "it is indeed a beautiful world, but nothing is as beautiful as my own little piece of it."

◇◇◇

In the history of France in the years of occupation, the pages devoted to Savoie will count among the most proud and most glorious.

For the most beautiful thing in that most beautiful of landscapes—was the attitude of the Savoyard people.

The whole region maintained its independent spirit and continued to offer assistance and hospitality to those pouring in, seeking refuge in ever greater numbers.

The maquis country filled with people resisting being drafted into work for the Germans, from all corners of France, and individual homes provided shelter to the persecuted.

At the same time, the Gestapo and the French Militia continued to arrive, setting up everywhere.

Developments in other *départements* suggested that in Savoie the Italian Occupation would be replaced by the German authorities any day.

Vichy's influence continued to grow . . .

In May 1943, a group of refugees had, as usual, gone to register their presence at the police station. They were arrested on the spot and incarcerated in the cellars of the town hall, pending orders from Vichy.

The Viennese woman was informed; her husband and father were among those arrested. Panic-stricken, she hastened to the town hall, to the prefecture of police, to the gendarmerie, and returned to the town hall in tears . . . A French official, seeing no other possible solution, advised her to try the last resort: an appeal to the Italian occupying forces.

She went to the hotel where the commission had its headquarters. After asking her to wait, the Commandant climbed into his car, went to the prefecture, and ordered the immediate release of all detainees. The order was hurriedly carried out. Following this success, the Viennese lady came to be known as the "Ambassadress." And on more than one occasion, she lodged appeals on behalf of prisoners, those who had been released and fugitives.

She was certainly not lacking in resourcefulness.

Sitting by the lake one afternoon, I noticed a young woman who looked familiar. When she reached me, I recognized her— the Viennese lady! But how she had changed! Looking svelte as she walked in her high heels, there was no longer any sign of pregnancy . . .

"Congratulations! Did you have a boy or a girl?" I asked her when she sat down beside me.

"If I'd had to give birth, it would have been all over with a very long time ago," she replied, laughing. "No, no, the fact is, I was never pregnant at all! The camp doctor, a decent Frenchman— how many poor wretches did he save at that time!—wrote me a certificate to say I was pregnant to avoid my being deported. The rest of it was all due to an excellent belt, an enormous—and now unnecessary—affair."

I was staggered.

This subterfuge was but one of a thousand and one methods employed to escape persecution.

In May, the local police were compelled, by order of the Vichy government, to stamp "*Jew*" on the documents of Jewish French citizens and foreigners alike.

There was nothing for it but to escape, no matter what, before this branding made any travel impossible.

Once again, the only way out was to make a run for it.

But at the Swiss Consulate in Annemasse, I learned that the anticipated visa had not yet arrived.

I went into hiding once more.

XV

Heading for Switzerland

Eight days later, the renewed visa arrived . . . it was valid for another month, and that was all!

Once again I was given the necessary instructions. Before I could do anything, I had to secrete myself away in the convent immediately to avoid the Militia, who were conducting roundups.

As my identity papers still made no mention of race, I could move about without any imminent danger.

From the convent, I went to the designated inn at seven o'clock in the evening. There, I asked after customs officer H——.

Originally from the hamlet of E——, and suspected— although not yet proven—of having assisted the escape of men seeking to avoid forced labor in Germany, the customs officer continued to devote himself to the cause, notwithstanding his own compromised situation.

He had already been told I was coming.

A cheerful, courteous fellow, he greeted me good-humoredly.

He introduced me to the innkeeper as his wife's friend who was coming to holiday with them for a month.

"Ah! So that's how it is," said the innkeeper's wife with far too much conviction, or so it seemed to me.

The customs officer offered me something to eat and drink. I noticed he enjoyed considerable popularity in the place. By the way I was served, I realized that here, as in most Savoyard establishments, people were aware of "the situation" and looked sympathetically on Monsieur H—— and those in his care.

However, when two gendarmes came in and sat down not far from us, my confidence deserted me. I soon realized these two jovial fellows were paying no attention to me: they approached our table to exchange a few words with some guests, brushing past me almost, but without even seeing me.

I whispered to the customs officer that I was feeling uncomfortable; he replied that we still had to wait for his son. "He'll have his baccalaureate soon, you know!" he added proudly. His son arrived a few minutes later.

The lad was about sixteen or seventeen, skittish, with a schoolboy's cap pulled down over his eyes and books under his arm. He had an arrogant manner and seemed disdainful of those around him. He gestured to us and we stood up.

We were off.

On the way, I heard the schoolboy whispering to his father, who appeared to be defending himself. The son was muttering:

"You wait until you hear what Mum has to say."

"What's done is done," answered the father categorically.

We had four miles ahead of us and were walking along next to strands of barbed wire. The customs officer pointed out to me the position of gates in certain places that were regularly used by the Savoyard and Swiss population who lived along the border. Padlocked at night and open during the day, they had been used for many an escape, and were strictly monitored by German and Italian soldiers and by the French Militia.

The customs officer said the word "Militia" in a very particular way, with an expression of deep disgust.

I had, on several occasions, noticed that this term, even then, had a deeply pejorative meaning for many French people.

The gendarme who had been present when we were transferred to the jail had said: "We're not the Militia, you know." Another had insisted: "I hope nobody here takes us for one of the Militia!"

At the time I had not quite appreciated the significance of this distinction.

The customs officer's wife greeted me without enthusiasm, which I could not hold against her since her husband was already compromised and in danger.

The budding scholar was openly sulking. He launched headlong into an argument that he had started. He criticized his father for his anti-German opinions, his lack of caution, and his opportunism.

I spent a sleepless night under that roof, worrying about the days ahead. To bolster my spirits, I told myself that making it to Switzerland would, as well as leading me to safety, allow me to make contact with my mother and the rest of my relatives.

I made great plans . . .

Day was breaking: a dazzlingly beautiful June day.

◇◇◇

The customs officer's wife had been keen to see me leave and she accompanied me a little way.

We were walking on higher ground, and below me I could see the national highway, with loops of barbed wire, particularly dense in this area, stretching alongside into the distance.

In the daylight I could better make out the placement of the gates in the wire, but also the sentries posted every five hundred to a thousand feet, dressed in green, feathers in their hats, rifles slung over their shoulders—Italians! They stood about, leaned against a tree, sat on the slope, or paced backward and forward.

I parted ways with Madame H—— not far from a viaduct. Now I had to follow the main road and find an opening through the wire.

As I headed into danger for the third time, I nonetheless savored the peacefulness of the early morning hour.

Keenly aware of the painful burden of my imminent separation, I said my farewells to the mountains, to the meadows and fields, to the peaceful village, to this vast horizon, to France.

The thought of having to cross her borders unlawfully, like a criminal, filled me with sadness.

To pluck up courage, I recalled all the suffering I had endured, almost more than any human being could bear, but at the same time, I remained profoundly conscious of France's own terrible misfortunes and her complete subjugation.

Suddenly, I became aware of a growing feeling within—a heartrending longing for this country I was leaving behind.

◇◇◇

A farmer was busy cutting grass along the edge of the road.

"Lovely weather," I said to him, setting my bundle down at my feet and wiping my forehead.

"Yes, yes, it's a lovely day," he replied.

"Tell me, friend, is the gate open?" I whispered, not beating around the bush.

Without interrupting his work, he calmly moved away, then returned.

"It's open, but it has been raining, and it looks like it might be jammed," he said, without raising his head.

"What to do?" I thought, and I could feel the panic rising.

"Should I go?" I asked the question of the farmer, looking for some final word of encouragement.

"Go! But do it quickly . . . Courage!"

And continuing on with his work, he took a few more steps.

"It's now or never!" a voice cried out to me, the voice of every straining inch of my willpower, and I made a dash for it.

The gate was well and truly jammed.

I shook it with all my strength.

A furtive glance, instinctively, toward the sentry . . .

An Italian soldier was rushing in my direction!

Feverishly, hardly thinking, I clambered awkwardly over the obstacle—and threw myself onto the other side!

Barbed wire tore at my clothes as I fell. I struck the ground . . .

Almost immediately, a shot rang out.

Another soldier was approaching me now, and he too was running—rifle in hand!

Lying on the ground, stunned, I waited for him, resigned.

"Stand up, madame, you're not injured. I saw the Italian shoot into the air," said the soldier in French as he helped me to my feet.

"Where am I?"

"Come, now! You're in Switzerland, aren't you?"

Only then did I understand, and a flood of emotion washed over me: joy, hope, immense relief . . .

I was in Switzerland, I was saved!

I started to walk, while trying to staunch the blood that was flowing freely from my legs and hands. At the same time, I tried to rearrange my ripped clothes.

All at once, the tension drained from me.

I was crying . . . Quietly, the tears I had for so long held back started to flow . . . they felt like a hot spring flooding my face. I swallowed those bitter tears and, as I wept, I felt a crushing weight lift.

The Swiss soldier walked discreetly on ahead of me, carrying the pitiable bundle of belongings that had been my companion on my successive attempts to flee. In it was everything I had taken with me from France, save my grieving and deathly tired heart . . .

FIN

Chronology

July 14, 1889   Birth of Frymeta Idesa Frenkel, known as
Françoise Frenkel, at Piotrków, near Łódź, in
Poland.

Prior to 1914   Paris. Studying for a degree in arts at the
Sorbonne.

1919   Internship at a bookshop on Rue Gay-Lussac.

1921   Françoise Frenkel, together with her husband,
Simon Raichenstein, sets up the first French
bookshop in Berlin: La Maison du Livre.*

1933   In November, Simon Raichenstein goes into
exile in France. Françoise Frenkel henceforth
assumes sole responsibility for the bookshop.

---

* See Corine Defrance, La *"Maison du Livre français"* à Berlin (1923–1933) et la poli-
tique française du livre en Allemagne in Hans-Manfred Bock and Gilbert Krebs, Échanges
culturels et relations diplomatiques: Presences culturelles à Berlin au temps de la République
de Weimar, Paris: Presses de la Sorbonne nouvelle, 2005.

July 1939	Françoise Frenkel leaves Berlin shortly before the declaration of war and settles in Paris, where she remains for nine months.*
May 28, 1940	She flees Paris for the Southern Zone (*la zone sud*) and leaves her trunk for safekeeping at the Colisée et Champs-Élysées storage depot.
December 1940	Arrival in Nice. In February 1941, she takes a room at the hotel La Roseraie.
July 1942	Simon Raichenstein is rounded up in Paris. On July 24, he is deported from Drancy and dies on August 19 in Auschwitz-Birkenau, Poland.†
August 26, 1942	Roundup in Nice and in the Southern Zone. Françoise Frenkel finds refuge at the hairdressing salon owned by the Mariuses (12 Rue Saint-Philippe, between Rue de France and the Promenade des Anglais).
November 14, 1942	The Gestapo confiscates the trunk, which has been in storage at the Colisée storage depot for two years.
December 1942	Françoise Frenkel leaves Nice and attempts to cross into Switzerland. She is arrested and incarcerated in Annecy. She is tried and acquitted.

---

* When she files her claim for compensation in 1959, she dates her arrival as at "the first half of July 1939." See the annexed document, at p. 261. In the book, Françoise Frenkel gives a different date: August 27, 1939.

† Inscribed on the Wall of Names in the Shoah Memorial in Paris.

June 1943	Françoise Frenkel crosses the Franco-Swiss border unlawfully. That same year, she starts work on *No Place to Lay One's Head* (*Rien où poser sa tête*).
September 1945	*Rien où poser sa tête* is published by Éditions Jeheber (Geneva).
End of 1945	Likely return of Françoise Frenkel to Nice.
1958	Françoise Frenkel lodges a claim for compensation for the confiscation of her trunk by the Gestapo.
January 18, 1975	Françoise Frenkel dies in Nice.

DOSSIER

La Maison du Livre

"... increasing customer numbers forced me to consider expanding, and the bookshop moved to the capital's fashionable quarter." (p. 8)

Number 39a Passauer Strasse, where the bookstore La Maison du Livre used to be, no longer exists. It was located to the left of the white art nouveau building pictured. In its place stand the buildings of the KaDeWe department store, which were bombed in 1943 and rebuilt and expanded in 1950.

La Maison du Livre is the first French bookstore in Berlin. It opens in 1921 and is managed by Françoise Frenkel and her husband, Simon Raichenstein. Like Frenkel herself, he too studied in Paris prior to the First World War, first at the École Supérieure d'Aeronautique in 1913, then at the École Spéciale de Mécanique et d'Électricité.

From its first location at 13 Kleiststrasse, the bookstore moves to 27 Passauer Strasse and then to number 39a in the same street, where the Charlottenburg, Schöneberg, and Wilmersdorf districts meet, and where it becomes an almost obligatory landmark for French writers of the interwar period who are passing through Berlin. Jules Chancel recounts that "Madame Raichenstein . . . wanted her bookstore to be a centre for French thought."*

In 1933, in a document emanating from the Department of French Works Abroad (*Service des oeuvres françaises à l'étranger*, or *SOFE*), we learn that in that same year, the French Embassy rejects "an application for an extraordinary grant" for La Maison du Livre, which is under threat of bankruptcy "as a result of developments."† A letter from Henri Jourdan of the Institut Français reports, however, that if the "lady" from the bookstore has been "boycotted," it is not because "she is Jewish" but rather because "she is being criticized for propagating French culture."‡ On May 10, 1933, Simon Raichenstein obtains a Nansen passport.§ He leaves Berlin for Paris for the last time on November 9.

Françoise Frenkel runs La Maison du Livre for another five years. In the summer of 1939, she abandons her bookshop and her apartment "as they are"¶ and goes into exile in Paris.

---

* See Jules Chancel, *Dix ans après: un mark = six francs,* Fayard,1928, pp. 166–67.

† *SOFE* (*Service des oeuvres françaises à l'étranger*), vol. 269, handwritten note marked "Raichenstein," undated. MAE [Ministère des Affaires Étrangers]/La Courneuve.

‡ Archives of the Ministère des Postes, French Embassy in Berlin 1915/1939, Series B, vol. 463, note of the Institut Français in Berlin dated April 15, 1933, on the current state of "*oeuvres françaises*" [French businesses] in Berlin. MAE/Nantes. Correspondence cited by Corine Defrance, *La "Maison du Livre français" à Berlin* (1923–1933).

§ Named after its originator, Fridtjof Nansen, High Commissioner for Refugees for the League of Nations. Created in July 1922, the Nansen passport was an identification and travel document intended for refugees and stateless persons.

¶ See the "Statutory Declaration" on p. 256.

Paris, Colisée Storage Depot

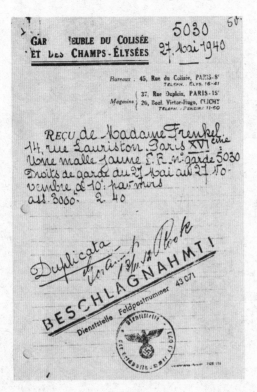

"Yet now that trunk, which had so miraculously survived, had been confiscated by the Germans in Paris on the grounds of my race. I had just learned as much from a postcard sent to me in Avignon by the storage depot." (p. 6)

Receipt for Françoise Frenkel's trunk from the Colisée et Champs-Élysées storage depot, dated May 27, 1940. Subsequent stamp noting confiscation by the German army affixed in 1942.

This receipt appears among the documents contained in the compensation claim filed by Françoise Frenkel after the war.

Nice, La Roseraie Hotel

"The hotel, La Roseraie, should have been called Noah's Ark.

It was home to survivors from the most diverse nationalities and social classes. They were a disparate lot indeed, united by their shared waiting for peace." (p. 90)

La Roseraie as it is today, located at 10 Avenue Depoilly in Nice, a cul-de-sac lined with Belle Epoque villas. Françoise Frenkel lived here from February 1941 to August 26, 1942.

Marius, Hairdressing Salon

Maniglier et Cantol, Sté méridionale d'affichage et de régie et vente d'immeubles, 11, r. St-François-de-Paule. 882.11
Manini (E.), bouch., charcut. fine, 70, boul. Carnot........... 66.88
Manini fils cadet, entrepr. plomb., zing., 44, bd Ste-Agathe.. 61.41
Manoli (G.), doct. méd., ch. des Serres................. 755.51
Manset (H.), villa Manset, av. Paul-Arène.................. 826.27
Mautica (J.), 8, r. Georges-Ville..................... 820.14
Manuel (H.), ing., villa St-Léger, cité Villermont.......... 818.06
Manufacture Belfor, 7, av. Gloria................... 753.65
Manufacture française d'armes et cycles de Saint-Etienne, 21, boul. Gambetta. 854.10
Manufacture italo-française, confections, 22 ter, r. de France. 866.14
Manus, bijoutier, 68, av. de la Victoire—................. 833.39
Manutention militaire....................... 825.56
Manzoni-Fluatz, antiquités, 2, r. Maccarani.................. 614.03
— succurs., prom. des Anglais prolongée, rd-point Champ- de-Courses. 754.78
Maquet, grav.-maroqu., 16, av. de Verdun............. 832.01
Marassi, docteur médecin, 53, av. Maréchal-Foch........... 870.09
Marbre (Tout en), 176, rte de Turin................ 826.82
Marcel Mézin, peintre en lettres, 28, r. Lamartine......... 870.72
Marcelet (Henri), chimiste, 4, r. Lépante................. 834.38
Marcellesi, représ., 23, rte de Levens.................. 896.01
Marcellin frères, confiseurs, 5, r. de Dijon.............. 834.48
Marcellini (H.), 1, r. Lamartine.................. 824.03
Marcellini (G.) et Cie, huiles d'olive, 18 bis, r. Em.-Philibert. 61.91
Marck (G.), doct. méd., 12. boul. Raimbaldi............ 802.35
Marchand (M. et Mme), Lauradour (Mme de)............. 67.98
Marchand (Jules), villa Lolette, boul. de Cambrai.......... 752.40
Marché de la Bonneterie, 26, r. Pertinax................. 852.35
Marcheteau, photogr., 6, r. J.-Serraire.................. 847.37
Marchi (Mme M.), 9, r. de Paris.................. 802.08
Marchio (A.), chevillard, 5, av. de Savoie............... 851.68
Marchio (Mme M.), 19, r. St-François-de-Paule.......... 844.67
Marchio frères, fleurs en gros, 11, r. Saint-François-de-Paule. 848.55
Marchio frères, fleuristes, 9, r. Saint-François-de-Paule..... 848.40
Marchisio et Morra, entr. de menuis., 90, r. Roquebillière.. 831.50
Marcobelli (M.), cycles, 12, r. Dalpozzo............... 861.81
Marcou (V.), homme de lettres, pavillon Marie-Louise, av. Gus- tavin. 63.83
Maréchaux (E.), villa Mondragon, av. Primerose........... 815.78
Marengo, pap. peints, 4, r. Lépante................. 842.92
Maret (J.), avocat, 52, r. Giofiredo................ 816.26
Margaria (F.), fruits et prim., 4, boul. Armée-des-Alpes..... 60.24
Margoliès (Mme), doctoresse en médec., 35, r. Rossini....... 837.11
Marguerite, 7, r. du Congrès.................. 867.14
Marguerite Landelle, corsets, lingerie, 7, r. Maréchal-Pétain. 844.69
Mari (A.), représentant, 7, pl. Cassini.................. 860.06
Mari (G.), 59, av. de la Lanterne.................. 754.30
Mari (V.), transp. intern., 27, r. Paganini................ 874.87
Mari fils et Dalbera, vins en gros, 60, boul. Risso........... 826.65
Maria (A.), couronnes mortuaires, 10, r. Hôtel-des-Postes..... 849.68
Maria (F.), représ. comm., 30, r. Verzier................ 823.47
Maria (G.), villa Nelly, r. Jacques-Bounin............... 805.72
Maria (P.), épicerie, 57, av. Cyrille-Besset............. 890.73
Maria frères, boulang-pâtiss., 48, r. de la République........ 868.01
Maria et Dotta, bobinage, moteur, 1, r. Châteauneuf........ 896.62
Mariage (J.-L.), adm. dél. Cie T.N.L., villa les Violettes, ch. des Crêtes. 61.64
Mariani (A.), tailleur p. dames, 4, r. de Russie............ 61.64
Mariani (A.), fabr. galneries, 34, r. Escarène............. 833.86
Mariani, électr., 109, r. de France.................. 851.93
Mariano, coiff., parfum., 9, r. Massena................ 853.22
Mariau (Albert), doct. chirurg., 18, av. Auber............. 843.96
Mariau (Philippe), doct. chirurg., 18, av. Auber........... 843.15
Marientross, 21, r. Verdi.................. 810.29
Marie-Dyl (Sté An.), 42, boul. Joseph-Garnier............. 861.18
Marie-Thérèse, couture, Jardin-du-Roi-Albert-Ier......... 875.56
Marine Nationale, inscript. marit., 12, qu. Lunel.......... 60.45
Marine Nationale, 16, boul. Dubouchage................. 861.80
Marinelli (G.), 9, boul. Armée-des-Alpes.............. 62.05
Marinette, coiffure p. dames, 3, av. Auber............. 862.13
Marini (M.), 26, av. Maréchal-Foch................. 891.25
Marino (P.), doct. en méd., 54, r. Verdi.............. 828.42
Marion (Mme), infirmière, 10, r. de Paris.............. 817.74
Marius, salon de coiffure, 12, r. Saint-Philippe.......... 856.76
Marjollet, villa Agnès-Paulette, av. René-Maurice........... 881.37
Marjoulet (Mme la Générale), 11, r. du Congrès........... 854.23
Marlot (J.), industr., 28, boul. Carabacel............. 887.96
Marly's, cristaux, cadeaux, 25, prom. des Anglais............ 872.11
Marolles (H.), 6, r. Meyerber.................. 813.93

Maroquinerie de l'Opéra, 12, av. de la Victoire............ 878.88
Marouani (D.), 10, r. Verdi.................. 891.28
Marquis, herboristerie, 6o, r. Bonaparte............. 60.96
Marquise de Sévigné (A la), 16, av. de Verdun........... 826.91
Marquise de Sévigné (A la), 8, av. de la Victoire........... 855.01
Marre (G.), pédic. chiropod., 20, r. Maréchal-Pétain......... 870.87
Marrot, pharmacien, 9 bis, r. François-Guizol............. 67.63
Mars (B.), couronnes mort., 4, r. Alex.-Mari.......... 837.09
Mars (F.), 10, r. Neville-Chamberlain............... 867.03
Mars, vins en gros, 6, r. Defly.................. 823.29
Mars frères et Cotto, constr. mécan., 17, r. Bavastro....... 61.18
Marsigliotti frères, entr. trav. publi., villa Les Roses, av. Isnard. 755.89
Marsollet (Raoul), 15, r. Alex.-Mari................. 836.22
Martel, mach. à écrire, 8, r. Rancher............... 642.63
Martelly (G.), représ., 15, r. Gustave-Deloye............. 853.38
Marthe, coiffeur, 20, r. de la Buffa.................. 802.48
Martin, villa les Oliviers, av. du Mesnil, Fabron.......... + 809.01
Martin, notaire, 51, av. de la Victoire............... 754.93
Martin, café, thés, 26, qu. Saint-Jean-Baptiste............ 827.37
Martin (A.), 4, r. de Paris (nov. à avril inclus)........... 814.62
Martin (A.), corsetière, 5, r. Bardon................ 856.93
Martin-Cauquil (S.), 53, rte de Marseille.............. 751.74
Martin (Charles), entrepreneur, 34, boul. de Cambral....... 796.38
Martin (Claude) fils, représ. comm., 15, r. Barla............ 66.33
Martin (D.), court. huiles, 14, qu. Saint-Jean-Baptiste...... 898.96
Martin (E.), fleuriste, 14, r. du Congrès............. 837.75
Martin (G.), agent comm., villa Calendal, Parc Ferber...... 758.88
Martin (Gaston), fleuriste, 28, r. Hôtel-des-Postes......... 813.63
Martin (G.), élect., 52, r. Assalit................. 820.14
Martin (H.), élect., 5a, r. Assalit................. 848.65
Martin (H.), mécanique, élect., 4, r. Xavier-de-Maistre..... 850.80
Martin (J.), architecte, 16, r. Dante................ 816.44
Martin (J.), cuplier, 57, boul. Victor-Hugo.............. 805.98
Martin (Mme H.), 2, r. Rossini................ 835.09
Martin (Mlle), huiles, 28, r. Giofiredo............. 816.15
Martin (Mlle M.), sage-femme, 30, r. Reine-Jeanne........ 854.79
Martin (Pierre), villa Turquoise, av. Caravadossi........... 826.77
Martin (P.), mécanicien, 16a, av. California............. 796.33
*MARTIN ET CIE (Entrepr. Charles), bureaux, 13g bis, rte de Marseille. 757.20
Martin (Urbain), ingénieur, 29, av. de Montclair.......... 890.47
Martin (Victor), archit. expert, 27, av. Villermont......... 854.74
Martin-Bermond, expédit. fleurs, 5, boul. Magnan.......... 792.09
Martin-Gout, art. voyages, maroqu., 55, r. Giofiredo........ 884.01
Martin-Milon, 16, r. Préfecture.................. 807.55
Martin Pyns, villa Henriette, av. La Madelon............. 808.65
Martina, entrepr. serrurerie, 20, r. Ferber............. 755.87
Martina et Iotta, plomb. sanit., 32, r. Escarène.......... 848.85
Martinelli (Ch.), entrep. maçon., 39, boul. Carlone......... 754.79
Martinelli (J.), 20, r. Berlioz.................. 801.92
Martinetti (A.), représ., 13, boul. de Cimies........... 877.22
Martinetti (F.), Palais du Jardin, pl. Cais-de-Gilette........ 63.13
Martinetti (Jean) fils, tailleur, 17, r. de la Préfecture....... 881.30
Martinetti et fils, plongeurs tailleurs, 11, r. de la Préfecture... 843.76
Martini (Ch.), avocat, 5, r. Galléan................. 876.62
Martini (P.), chirurg. dent., 6, r. Defly.............. 864.24
MARTINI ET CIE (Sté anon.), transp. *déménagements*, 17, av. Thiers, + 829.63
— dépôt transp., r. du Docteur-Pierre-Richielmi.......... 64.40
— agent en douanes, 4, qu. Papacino.............. 60.96
— *Service du camionnage et laclage P. L. M.......... 820.29
— *Service postal Cie Fraissinet.................. 62.21
— *Antibes, boul. Albert-Ier, demander le 412.63 Antibes.
— *Antibes, gare 410.31 Juan-les-Pins.
— *Breil (agence en douanes), demander le 16 Breil.
Martini et Rossi, vermouth, 40, boul. Gambetta........... 898.74
Martini et Russo, aliment. gén., 26, av. Malausséna......... 880.76
Martino (Mlle M.), 30, r. des Ponchettes............. 893.34
Martino (B.), villa L's Palmiers, Parc Chambrun........... 876.46
Martinon (J.), 10, r. de la République.............. 830.84
Martinon, change, bourse, 25, av. de la Victoire.......... + 849.39
Marty, négoc., 4, r. du Pont-Vieux.................. 848.72
Marty, représent. comm., 45, av. Borriglione............ 802.60
Marverti (G.), 14, imp. St-Laurent................ 755.35
Marve (L.-F.), mat. prem. aromat., 51, av. Domaine-du-Piol. 808.96
Mary (Louis), 54, r. Gioffredo.................. 894.11
Mary (P.), fourn. pour tailleur, 52, r. Hôtel-des-Postes....... 825.80
Maryland, 177, promenade des Anglais.............. 756.78
Maruat (M.), avoué, 23, av. de la Victoire............ 835.60
Marzi (F.), plombier, 135, r. de France............... 855.90

MAISON MARS Travaux sur commande — Spécialité Plantes perles, garnitures tombeaux   Téléphone :
COURONNES MORTUAIRES, 4, rue Alexandre-Mari (Anc. r. du Palais) NICE   837.03

"*I scanned the avenue, the little laneways, the houses, shops, and villas, searching instinctively for somewhere to take cover.*

My eyes fell on a shop window: MARIUS—HAIRDRESSING SALON." (p. 103)

Official telephone directory of the Alpes-Maritimes *département*, 1941 edition, containing the following entry: Marius, hairdressing salon, 12 Rue Saint-Philippe, tel. 856.76.

FRANÇOISE FRENKEL

RIEN OÙ POSER
SA TÊTE

GENÈVE
Edition J.-H. Jeheber S. A.
6, rue du Vieux-Collège, 6

En France : Edition Jeheber, Annemasse (Haute-Savoie)

Title page of original edition of *Rien où poser sa tête*, 1945.

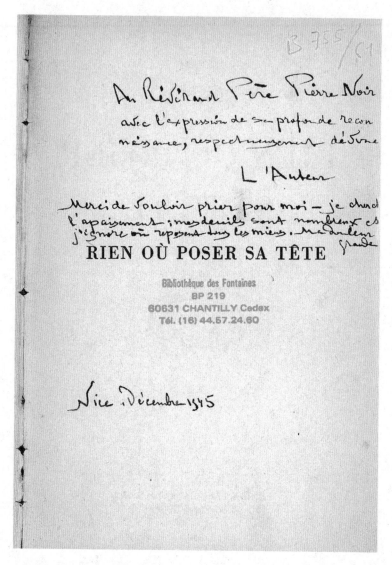

Françoise Frenkel's handwritten dedication to Father Noir in a copy of *Rien où poser sa tête*.

*To Reverend Father Pierre Noir, with my deepest gratitude,
respectfully yours, The Author.*

*I would be so grateful for your prayers—I seek inner
peace: I am grieving for so many and know not where my
family have been laid to rest. How great is my suffering. Nice.
December 1945."* (Lyon Municipal Library, classification:
SJ B755/61.)

The inscription suggests that Françoise Frenkel returned to
Nice to live from the end of 1945.

An article

Publications reçues

Françoise FRENKEL: *Rien où poser sa tête*. Edit.
J.-H. Jeheber S. A. Genève.

Les récits dont l'action se situe dans le cadre
de la guerre ont entre eux une tragique parenté.
C'est pourquoi, en lisant « Rien où poser sa
tête », on pense à « Je suis une vraie Norvégienne », malgré la différence des personnages
et des situations.

Françoise Frenkel, d'origine polonaise, était
directrice d'une librairie française, à Berlin,
lorsque les événements de 1939 l'obligèrent à
fuir. Ne pouvant gagner sa patrie, elle se réfugia
en France, à Paris, où elle avait fait ses études.
Mais bientôt l'exode l'entraîna vers le Midi. A
partir de ce moment, les péripéties se succédèrent
vécues douloureusement, « sans rien où poser sa
tête...» Pourtant de lumineux rayons se glissent
parmi les images de misère, et nous en savons
gré à l'auteur. Pas de plaintes, des faits rap-
portés avec décence et mesure, d'une manière très
vivante. Françoise Frenkel ne serait-elles pas
une des « héroïnes inconnues » ?   R. G.

Article published in *Le Mouvement féministe: organe officiel des
publications de l'Alliance nationale des sociétés féminines suisses* in
1946.

The only known review of the book.

TRANSLATED TEXT:

Publications Received

Françoise Frenkel: *Rien où poser sa tête* [No Place to Lay One's Head].
Publishers: J.-H. Jeheber S.A. Geneva.

Narratives set in the context of war share a tragic parentage. Which is why, when reading *No Place to Lay One's Head*, one is reminded of *Je suis une vraie Norvégienne* [*Norway Is My Country**], despite differences in characters and circumstances.

Françoise Frenkel, a woman of Polish origin, was running a French bookstore in Berlin when the events of 1939 forced her to flee. Unable to return to her homeland, she took refuge in France—Paris—where she had studied. But the exodus soon forced her south to the Midi. From that moment onward, the twists and turns of Fate follow one after the other, grievously endured "with no place to lay one's head . . ." Yet rays of light illuminate the images of misery, and for that we must be grateful to the author. There are no complaints, just facts, reported with a sense of decency and in a measured but most lively fashion. Is Françoise Frenkel not one of our "unsung heroines"?

R.G.

---

*A reference to Synnøve Christensen's (a pseudonym of the writer and actor Margit Lindegärd Solem) autobiographical account of life under German Occupation in Norway, *Ja, jag är en norsk kvinna*, 1943, published in English as *Norway Is My Country*.

Compensation claim

Anmeldung

von rückerstattungsrechtlichen Geldansprüchen gegen das Deutsche Reich und gleichgestellte Rechtsträger*)

Bundesgesetz zur Regelung der rückerstattungsrechtlichen Geldverbindlichkeiten des Deutschen Reichs und gleichgestellter Rechtsträger

(Bundesrückerstattungsgesetz — BRüG —)
vom 19. Juli 1957
(Bundesgesetzbl. I S. 734)

Der Hauptreuhänder für Rückerstattungsvermögen
- 1 JULI 1958

Der Haupttreuhänder
für Rückerstattungsvermögen
Berlin W 30, Nürnberger Str. 53-55
- Zentralanmeldeamt -

Reg. Nr.: G/ 6380 /F

A. Personalangaben
Anlagen

1. Personalangaben des Antragstellers

a) Familienname **F R E N K E L**
(bei Frauen auch Geburtsname) geb. FRENKEL

b) Vorname Françoise Frymeta

c) jetzt wohnhaft NIZZA(Frankreich),1 avenue de Bellet.

d) Geburtsdatum und Ort Piotrkow(Polen).

e) Staatsangehörigkeit FRANZOESISCH.

f) Beruf Vormals Buchhändlerin,jetzt Schriftstellerin.

g) Wohnort (ständiger Aufenthalt) PARIS(17e)Rue Colonel MOLL, 19.
im Zeitpunkt der Entziehung

h) Wohnsitz oder Aufenthalt oder geschäftliche Hauptniederlassung des Antragstellers im Gebiet der jetzigen Bundesrepublik Deutschland oder in den jetzigen Westsektoren von Berlin zu irgendeinem Zeitpunkt während der Zeit vom 30. Januar 1933 bis 8. Mai 1945 von 1921-39 in Berlin,Passauerstr.39.

i) Wohnsitz im Jahre 1948 NIZZA,Franreich.

k) Angaben über die Antragsberechtigung, falls der Antragsteller nicht der Geschädigte ist: (Erbfolge, Abtretung u. dgl.)

---

*) Nach § 1 BRüG findet das Gesetz Anwendung auf rückerstattungsrechtliche Ansprüche gegen das Deutsche Reich einschließlich der Sondervermögen Deutsche Reichsbahn und Deutsche Reichspost.

Das Gesetz findet ferner Anwendung auf rückerstattungsrechtliche Ansprüche gegen 1. das ehem. Land Preußen, 2. das Unternehmen Reichsautobahnen, 3. die ehem. Nationalsozialistische Deutsche Arbeiterpartei (NSDAP), deren Gliederungen, deren angeschlossene Verbände und die sonstigen aufgelösten NS-Einrichtungen, 4. die Reichsvereinigung der Juden in Deutschland und den Auswanderungs-

"My great trunk, salvaged from Berlin, was put into storage in Paris."
(p. 40)

Form for Françoise Frenkel's compensation claim dated 1958.

TRANSLATED TEXT:

Nationality: French

Profession: formerly bookseller, currently author

Address: 1 Avenue de Bellet, Nice

Address at the time of events in question: 19 Rue du Colonel-Moll,
    Paris, 17th arrondissement

Subject of the claim: loss of items of luggage (see attached list)

Grounds of claim: seizure by the Gestapo

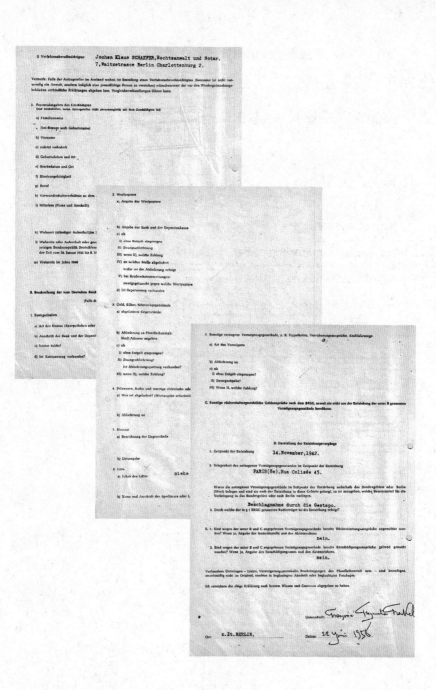

i) Verfahrensbevollmächtigter: **Jochen Klaus SCHAEFER,Rechtsanwalt und Notar.**
7,Waitzstrasse Berlin Charlottenburg 2.

Vermerk: Falls der Antragsteller im Ausland wohnt, ist Bestellung eines Verfahrensbevollmächtigten (hierunter ist nicht notwendig ein Anwalt, sondern lediglich eine prozessfähige Person zu verstehen) erwünscht; der vor den Wiedergutmachungsbehörden verbindliche Erklärungen abgeben bzw. Vergleichsverhandlungen führen kann.

2. Personalangaben des Geschädigten
(nur auszufüllen, wenn Antragsteller nicht personengleich mit dem Geschädigten ist)

a) Familienname

. (bei Frauen auch Geburtsname)

b) Vorname

c) zuletzt wohnhaft

d) Geburtsdatum und Ort

e) Sterbedatum und Ort

f) Staatsangehörigkeit

g) Beruf

h) Verwandtschaftsverhältnis zu dem

i) Miterben (Name und Anschrift)

k) Wohnort (ständiger Aufenthalt)

l) Wohnsitz oder Aufenthalt oder ganz jetzigen Bundesrepublik Deutschland der Zeit vom 30. Januar 1933 bis 8. M

m) Wohnsitz im Jahre 1943

3. Beschreibung der vom Deutschen Reich

(Falls d

1. Bankguthaben

a) Art des Kontos (Sparguthaben oder

b) Anschrift der Bank und der Deposit

c) letzter Saldo?

d) Ist Kontoauszug vorhanden?

2. Wertpapiere
a. Angabe der Wertpapiere

b) Angabe der Bank und der Depositenkasse
c) ob
I) ohne Entgelt eingezogen
II) Zwangsablieferung
III) wenn II), welche Zahlung
IV) an welcher Stelle abgeliefert
wofür ist die Ablieferung erfolgt
V) bei Reichsschatzanweisungen:
zwangsgetauscht gegen welche Wertpapiere
d) Ist Depotauszug vorhanden

3. Gold, Silber, Schmuckgegenstände
a) abgelieferte Gegenstände:

b) Ablieferung an Pfandleihanstalt:
Stadt/Adresse angeben
c) ob
I) ohne Entgelt eingezogen?
II) Zwangsablieferung?
Ist Ablieferungsquittung vorhanden?
III) wenn II), welche Zahlung?

4. Pelzwaren, Radio und sonstige elektrische ode
a) Was ist abgeliefert? (Wertangabe erforderli

b) Ablieferung an

5. Hausrat
a) Beschreibung der Gegenstände

b) Ortsangabe

6. Liste
a) Inhalt der Liste   siehe

b) Name und Anschrift des Spediteurs oder L

7. Sonstige entzogene Vermögensgegenstände, z. B. Hypotheken, Versicherungsansprüche, Kraftfahrzeuge
a) Art des Vermögens

b) Ablieferung an
c) ob
I) ohne Entgelt eingezogen?
II) Zwangsabgabe?
III) Wenn II, welche Zahlung?

C. Sonstige rückerstattungsrechtliche Geldansprüche nach dem BRüG, soweit sie nicht aus der Entziehung der unter B genannten Vermögensgegenstände herrühren.

D. Darstellung der Entziehungsvorgänge

1. Zeitpunkt der Entziehung   **14.November,1942.**

2. Belegenheit des entzogenen Vermögensgegenstandes im Zeitpunkt der Entziehung
PARIS(8e),Rue Colisée 45.

Waren die entzogenen Vermögensgegenstände im Zeitpunkt der Entziehung außerhalb des Bundesgebiets oder Berlin (West) belegen und sind sie nach der Entziehung in diese Gebiete gelangt, so ist anzugeben, welche Beweismittel für die Verlagerung in das Bundesgebiet oder nach Berlin vorliegen.

Beschlagnahme durch die Gestapo.
3. Durch welche der in § 1 BRüG genannten Rechtsträger ist die Entziehung erfolgt?

E. 1. Sind wegen der unter B und C angegebenen Vermögensgegenstände bereits Rückerstattungsansprüche angemeldet worden? Wenn ja, Angabe der Anmeldestelle und des Aktenzeichens.
nein.

2. Sind wegen der unter B und C angegebenen Vermögensgegenstände bereits Entschädigungsansprüche geltend gemacht worden? Wenn ja, Angabe des Entschädigungsamts und des Aktenzeichens.
nein.

Vorhandene Unterlagen – Listen, Versteigerungsprotokolle, Bescheinigungen der Pfandleihanstalt usw. – sind beizufügen, zweckmäßig nicht im Original, sondern in beglaubigter Abschrift oder beglaubigter Fotokopie.

Ich versichere die obige Erklärung nach bestem Wissen und Gewissen abgegeben zu haben.

Unterschrift:

Ort: z. Zt. BERLIN,   Datum:

252

Inventory of contents of trunk

Anlage zur Anmeldung von Rückerstattungsrechtlichen Ansprüchen gegen das Deutsche Reich (zu B. 6)   Frau Witwe F. FRENKEL geb. FRENKEL, wohnhaft in NIZZA/Frankreich, z. Zt. Berlin.

INHALTSVERZEICHNIS

des Maedlerkoffers, beschlagnahmt von der GESTAPO in PARIS am 14. November 1942 (aus Rassengründen), laut Bestätigung der Firma Garde-Meubles du Colisée in PARIS, 45 rue du Colisée (Lagerhaus).-

1)	ein Maedler-Rohrplattenkoffer mit Messingringen, innen Schubladen und 3 Abteilungen . . . . DM.	345,00
2)	ein NUTRIAPELZMANTEL dreiviertellang (Herpich Söhne). .	1.800,00
3)	ein Kostüm, Massarbeit ; ; ;	225,00
4)	ein Mantel mit Opossumkragen, Massarbeit	200,00
5)	zwei Wollkleider nach Mass, je 150.-	300,00
6)	ein schwarzer Regenmantel	45,00
7)	eine Halskette (Bernstein)	50,00
8)	ein Morgenrock Fa. Grünfeld	25,00
9)	drei Nachthemden mit Stickerei Fm. Grünfeld, je 25.+ . .	75,00
10)	drei Nachthemden mit Stickerei Fa. Grünfeld, je 30.- . .	90,00
11)	zwei Unterkleider, Kunstseide je 25.-	50,00
12)	ein Unterkleid, Kunstseide	40,00
13)	ein Regenschirm	22,00
14)	ein Sonnenschirm 'en tout-cas'	32,00
15)	drei Paar Lederschuhe (Stiller) .j e. 25.-	75,00
16)	eine Handtasche	35,00
17)	eine Aktenmappe	50,00
18)	ein Tauchsieder	12,00
19)	ein Heizkissen	18,00
20)	eine Daunendecke	230,00
21)	dazu frei bunte Ueberzüge à 35.-	105,00
22)	eine neue Erika-Portable Schreibmaschine	400,00
23)	eine neuwertige Universal-Portable Schreibmaschine	350,00
24)	die in den Ziehkästen und Schubladen befindlichen Handschuhe, Strümpfe, Spitzenkragen, Taschentücher usw. usw. . . ca.	300,00

Total : ... 4.874,00 D)

Inventory and estimated value of contents of Françoise Frenkel's trunk, annexed to compensation claim form dated 1958.

TRANSLATED TEXT:

Annexure to the Claim for Compensation brought against the German Reich on behalf of the widow, Frau F. FRENKEL née FRENKEL, domiciled in NICE/France, currently residing in Berlin.

DESCRIPTION OF CONTENTS

of the Mädler trunk confiscated by the GESTAPO in PARIS on 14 November 1942 (on the grounds of race), as confirmed by the Colisée storage depot business in PARIS, at 45 Rue du Colisée (Warehouse).

1. one Mädler canvas-and-cane-bound steamer trunk with brass fittings, internal drawers and 3 compartments — DM 345.00
2. one three-quarter length COYPU FUR COAT (Herpich Söhne) — 1,800.00
3. one suit—custom-made — 225.00
4. one coat with an opossum collar—custom-made — 200.00
5. two woolen dresses made-to-measure, 150.- each — 300.00
6. one black raincoat — 45.00
7. one necklace (amber) — 50.00
8. one dressing gown—Grünfeld — 25.00
9. three embroidered nightdresses—Grünfeld, 25.- each — 75.00
10. three embroidered nightdresses—Grünfeld, 30.- each — 90.00
11. two slips, rayon, 25.- each — 50.00
12. one rayon slip — 40.00
13. one umbrella — 22.00
14. one parasol — 32.00
15. three pairs of leather shoes (Stiller), 25.- each — 75.00
16. one handbag — 35.00
17. one briefcase — 50.00

18. one immersion heater   12.00
19. one electric heat pad   18.00
20. one duvet   230.00
21. covers for [the above] in various colors, 35.-each   105.00
22. one new "Erika" portable typewriter   400.00
23. one "Universal" portable typewriter, as new   350.00
24. contained in the compartments and drawers: gloves, stockings, lace collars, handkerchiefs, etc.   approx. 300.00

TOTAL: 4,874.00 DM

Statutory declaration dated 1959

In July 1959, Françoise Frenkel returns to Berlin to settle her claim for compensation. She makes a statutory declaration in the presence of a notary public, which is reproduced here. In 1960, she obtains compensation in the sum of 3,500 Deutschmarks from the Federal Republic of Germany.

einer eidesstattlichen Versicherung und wies sie auf die Straf-
barkeit nach den Bestimmungen des Aufenthalts- und des Heimat-
landes für den Fall der Abgabe einer vorsätzlich oder fahrlässig
falschen eidesstattlichen Versicherung hin.

Hierauf erklärte die Erschienene folgendes:

Im Juli 1939 mußte ich wegen rassischer Verfolgung Berlin verlassen und mich in das Ausland begeben. Ich besaß damals die
polnische Staatsangehörigkeit, und mir drohte wegen meiner jüdischen Abstammung sowieso die Zwangsausweisung. Ich wäre unter die Aktionen gegen die jüdischen Polen gefallen. - Ich erhielt von dem französischen Konsulat eine entsprechende War-
nung, da ich eine französische Buchhandlung unter dem Namen
MAISON DU LIVRE betrieb. Ich habe damals meine Buchhandlung
und auch meine Wohnung verlassen, wie sie waren, und mich nur
darauf beschränkt, das Notwendigste, das heißt persönliche Gegenstände in einem Koffer mitzuführen. Dieser Maedler-Koffer
hatte den Inhalt, den ich auf einer besonderen Liste angege-
ben habe. Dieser Koffer stellte also mein Umzugsgut dar.

Es gelang mir durch die Unterstützung meines Mitarbeiters,
Herrn Roland Weimar, den Koffer nach Paris aufzugeben, und
dort fand ich ihn nach meiner Ankunft wieder vor, und zwar
am Bahnhof. Ich kam in Paris in der ersten Juli-Hälfte 1939
an. Ich wohnte bei Freunden in Paris und hatte dort meinen
Koffer untergestellt.

Als dann im Laufe des deutsch-französischen Krieges Paris von
den deutschen Truppen bedroht wurde und der Kommandant von Paris alle Frauen und Kinder zum Verlassen der Stadt aufforderte,
fühlte auch ich mich veranlaßt, dieser Aufforderung Folge zu
leisten. Wenn ich auch inzwischen die französische Staatsangehörigkeit erworben hatte, so mußte ich doch wegen meiner jüdischen Abstammung und früheren polnischen Staatsangehörigkeit
die deutschen Truppen fürchten. Ich verließ also am 28. Mai
1940 Paris, nachdem ich am Tage zuvor, am 27. Mai 1940, bei
dem Lagerhaus GARDEMEUBLE du Colysée, 45 rue Colysée, Paris 8e,
den Koffer eingelagert hatte. Ich begab mich dann nach Süd-
frankreich.

Im Herbst 1942, und zwar im November erhielt ich von dem

3

Lagerhaus ein Schreiben, das mir von meinen französischen Freunden aus Paris nach Nizza nachgesandt worden war und in welchem mir mitgeteilt wurde, daß dort lagerndes jüdisches Eigentum von der deutschen Besatzungsmacht beschlagnahmt werden sollte. Ich wurde angefragt, ob ich die Möglichkeit hätte nachzuweisen, daß ich "arisch" sei, um mein Eigentum vor einer derartigen Beschlagnahme zu bewahren. Ich habe dieses Schreiben nicht beantwortet, weil ich jüdischer Abstammung bin und dadurch keine Aussicht bestand, eine Beschlagnahme des Koffers zu verhindern. Bei dieser Aktion in Paris hat es sich um eine allgemeine Aktion der Nazi-Behörden gegen jüdisches Eigentum gehandelt, und ich schließe daraus, daß meine Sachen mit denen anderer Juden in das Gebiet des ehemaligen Deutschen Reiches verbracht worden sind.

Wegen dieses Verlustes habe ich von keinem Staat, insbesondere weder von Frankreich noch von Polen irgendeine Entschädigung erhalten. Als ich nämlich diesen Schaden zunächst als Kriegsschaden bei einem französischen Amt anmelden wollte, hat man mir eine Entschädigung versagt mit der Begründung, daß es sich dabei nicht um einen üblichen Besatzungs- oder Kriegsschaden gehandelt habe, sondern um eine besondere Aktion gegen die Juden.

Die Richtigkeit vorstehender Angaben versichere ich an Eides Statt. Nach gewissenhafter Prüfung ist mir nichts bekannt, was der Richtigkeit meiner Angaben entgegensteht.

Ich beantrage, mir eine Ausfertigung - für die Wiedergutmachungsämter -, eine beglaubigte Abschrift - für den Senator für Finanzen Inneres - sowie mir eine einfache Abschrift zu erteilen.

Das Protokoll ist in Gegenwart des Notars mit den Ergänzungen und Berichtigungen vorgelesen, von der Beteiligten genehmigt und eigenhändig unterschrieben worden:

> gez. Frymeta Francoise F r e n k e l geb. Frenkel
> gez. S c h a e f e r , Notar

Kostenrechnung
Kostenordnung v. 26. 7. 57
Geschäftswert: 4.500,-- DM
Gebühr §§ 32, 49   30,-- DM
Umsatzsteuer   1,20 "
        zusammen 31,20 DM
        gez. Schaefer, Notar

- 4 -

Vorstehende, in die Urkundenrolle für das Jahr 1959 unter
Nummer 90 eingetragene Verhandlung wird hiermit für Frau
Frymeta Francoise F r e n k e l geborene Frenkel, zur
Zeit Berlin-Charlottenburg, Giesebrechtstraße 11, ausge-
fertigt.

Berlin, den 4. Juli 1959

                                    N o t a r

First certified copy

NOTARIZED

In Berlin on July 3, 1959
Before the undersigned Notary Public

JOCHEN KLAUS SCHAEFER

7 Waitztrasse, Berlin-Charlottenburg 4

Appearing today—and known to the Notary Public:

Frau Frymeta Françoise Frenkel, née Frenkel, domiciled at 1 Avenue de Bellet, Nice (Alpes-Maritimes) / France, currently residing at Pension Florian, 11 Giesebrechtstrasse, Berlin-Charlottenburg, has indicated that she wishes to file a statutory declaration with the Department of Reparation—Berlin in her proceedings pursuant to the federal law relating to compensation and in support of claim no. 62 WGA 1280/57.

The notary public has explained to the declarant the significance of a statutory declaration and noted that any false claim contained in such statement, whether intentionally or negligently made, shall be punishable according to the laws of the declarant's country of residence and country of origin.

Whereupon the declarant has made the following declaration:

In July 1939, I had to leave Berlin due to racial persecution and move abroad. At the time, I had Polish citizenship and was, in any event, at risk of forced deportation as a result of my Jewish background. I would have been exposed to measures targeting Polish

Jews. I received a warning to this effect from the French Consulate in light of the fact that I was running a French bookshop by the name of La Maison du Livre. I abandoned my bookstore as well as my apartment as they were, and limited myself to taking with me only what was strictly necessary, namely a trunk packed with my personal effects. I have set out the contents of this Mädler trunk in a separate list. The trunk therefore constituted all I took with me by way of personal possessions.

With the assistance of my work colleague, Herr Roland Weimar, I was able to arrange for the trunk to be sent to Paris, where I recovered it at the railway station upon my arrival. I arrived in Paris in the first half of July 1939. There I lived with friends, at whose home I stored the trunk.

When German troops threatened Paris in the war between France and Germany, and the Commander of Paris told all women and children to leave the city, I too felt obliged to comply with this demand. Despite having in the meantime acquired French citizenship, I was nonetheless fearful of the German troops due to my Jewish origins and previous Polish nationality. Thus, I departed Paris on May 28, 1940, having left my trunk the previous day, namely May 27, 1940, at the Colisée storage depot located at 45 Rue du Colisée, 75008, Paris. I then left for the south of France.

In the autumn of 1942, in November, I received correspondence in Nice from the storage depot, sent on to me by my French friends in Paris, in which I was informed of the imminent seizure of Jewish property by the German occupying forces. I was asked to prove, if I was so able, that I was "Aryan," in order to prevent my property from being seized. I did not respond to this letter as I am of Jewish origin, and thus had no prospect of preventing the seizure of my trunk. This action taken in Paris constituted part of a more general measure implemented by the National Socialist administration against Jewish property and I concluded that my belongings, along with those of other Jews, had been removed to the territory of the former German Reich.

I have not received any compensation for this loss from any state, and in particular neither from France nor from Poland. When I sought to declare this loss to French authorities as constituting war damage, I was refused compensation on the grounds that it did not constitute damage typically resulting from the Occupation or the war, but rather resulted from action taken specifically against Jews.

I hereby attest to the truthfulness of this statutory declaration. Having carefully reread the matters contained herein, I am not aware of anything which contravenes the truthfulness of my declarations.

I hereby seek to have drawn up: one certified original equivalent for the Department of Reparation, one certified executed copy for the Senator for Finances, as well as one simple copy for myself.

This statement, together with any additions or amendments, has been read aloud in the presence of the notary public, and approved and signed by the declarant.

Signed: Frymeta Françoise FRENKEL née Frenkel
Signed: SCHAEFER, Notary Public

The above declaration, recorded in the register of notarized deeds for the year 1959 under number 90, is drawn up on behalf of Frau Frymeta Françoise FRENKEL née Frenkel, currently residing at 11 Giesebrechtstrasse, Berlin-Charlottenburg.

Berlin, July 4, 1959

Statement of Herr Weymar

ROLAND WEYMAR
Buenos Aires
Superi 4299

Buenos Aires, den 30 juli 1959.

E R K L A E R U N G

Meine Mutter, meine Frau und ich wir waren mit Frau
Françoise Frenkel befreundet. Als sie im Jahre 1939
durch die drohende Deportation zur Flucht aus Berlin
veranlasst wurde, ging sie nach Paris.

Frau Françoise Frenkel verpackte ihre persönlichen
Gegenstände und Schreibmaschinen in einen Mädlerkof-
fer. Ich beförderte diesen Koffer zum Bahnhof Zoo
und habe ihn dort zum Versand gebracht. Den Versand-
schein händigte ich an Frau Françoise Frenkel aus.
Die Richtigkeit dieser Erklärung bestätigt an eides-
statt

Roland Weymar.

Vorstehende eigenhaendige Unterschrift de...
.......Roland..Weymar.....
.....................................Buenos Aires........
beglaubige ich hiermit auf Grund ihrer vor
mir erfolgten vollziehung. Anerkennung.
Buenos Aires, den

31. JULI 1959

Bezirk.Reg.   Konsulatssekretär
N° 1472/59   bei der Botschaft der Bundesrepublik Deutschland
Gebuehr Teil I gemäss § 97a Konsulargesetz

263

Statement of Herr Weymar, executed in Buenos Aires, Argentina, on July 30, 1959, and annexed to the claim for compensation dated July 1959.

TRANSLATED TEXT:

My mother, my wife, and I were friends of Madame Françoise Frenkel. In 1939, facing the threat of deportation, she was compelled to flee Berlin for Paris. Madame Frenkel packed her personal belongings and typewriters into a "Mädler" trunk. I took this trunk to the luggage dispatch office at Zoo station in Berlin. I then gave the dispatch docket to Madame Françoise Frenkel. I hereby attest to the truthfulness of these statements.

Roland Weymar

Last address

The last address of Françoise Frenkel: Villa Tanit, 5 Rue Alexandre Dumas, Nice.

Acknowledgments

Thanks to all who contributed to the publication of this edition. To Patrick Modiano for his interest in the project and for his preface to the work.

To Frédéric Maria for bringing the book to our attention and for the previously unpublished and illuminating Dossier.

To Michel Francesconi, who found a copy of *Rien où poser sa tête* in a bric-a-brac sale in Nice and who was the first to read it and share it.

To Valérie Scigala, who, through her blog, spread Françoise Frenkel's name on the internet.

To Élisabeth Beyer, manager of the Bureau du Livre in Berlin, for her constant, good-natured support.

To Sébastien Cadet at the Commission for the Compensation of Victims of Spoliation/Commission pour l'indemnisation des victimes de spoliations (CIVS) in Berlin for his research at the Berlin Landesarchiv (State Archive).

To Corine Defrance, who, in 2005, wrote what was then the only existing study on the La Maison du Livre bookstore, and who assisted with research.

To Anne Vijoux for her research in French libraries.

Finally, to Simon Srebrny, Irenka Taurek, and Peter Wechsler, relatives of Françoise Frenkel, whose memories and personal archives were of immeasurable assistance.

Photographic credits